A
USER's
Manual
for the
HUMAN
Body

A
USER'S
Manual
for the
HUMAN
Body

How Traditional Chinese Medicine
helps the body to heal itself

ALEX WU

H **H**
BOOKS
Hammersmith Health Books
London, UK

First published in Chinese in 2005 by Shengya, China
Published in English in 2019 by Hammersmith Health Books
 – an imprint of Hammersmith Books Limited
4/4a Bloomsbury Square, London WC1A 2RP, UK
www.hammersmithbooks.co.uk

Disclaimer: The information contained in this book is for educational purposes
only. It is the result of the study and experience of the author. Whilst the
information and advice offered are believed to be true and accurate at the
time of going to press, neither the author nor the publisher can accept any
legal responsibility or liability for any errors or omissions that may have been
made or for any adverse effects which may occur as a result of following the
recommendations given herein. Always consult a qualified medical practitioner
if you have any concerns regarding your health.

British Library Cataloguing in Publication Data: A CIP record of this book is
available from the British Library.

Print ISBN 978-1-78161-138-8
Ebook ISBN 978-1-78161-139-5

Commissioning editor: Georgina Bentliff
Designed and typeset by: Sylvia Kwan
Cover design by: Sylvia Kwan
Index: Hammersmith Health Books
Production: Helen Whitehorn, Path Projects Ltd
Printed and bound by: TJ International Ltd, Cornwall, UK

CONTENTS

About the Author vii

Introduction 1
    Traditional Chinese Medicine – the past and present 3
    Introducing *A User's Manual for the Human Body* 5

1. The point of view of a product designer 9
    Using a product designer's point of view to solve chronic
    illnesses: a simple example 13
    What is the voltage of the human body? 16

2. Body energy 21
    Five levels of body energy 23
    The common cold and TCM's theory of cold-temperature
    damage 29
    The removal of cold-temperature damage and the
    common cold 33
    Uncomfortable symptoms may not be diseases 35
    How to increase body energy and the importance of
        sleeping early 41

3. Traditional Chinese Medicine's understanding of how the human
    body functions 45
    System simplification 47
    The meridian is the passageway for human body fluid 54
    The self-healing system 60
    The logic of self-healing 63
    The concept of energy management 64

4. Enabling the self-healing system to cure psoriasis and stop
   hair loss...71
   Redefining the symptoms of psoriasis..75
   The path to curing psoriasis...75
   Hair loss: my own experience 78

5. Applying the principles of Traditional Chinese Medicine to
   treating obesity..83
   Poorly functioning heart and spleen systems are the main
   cause of obesity...86
   Activities or habits that may contribute to spleen weakness ...88
   Drinking iced water as a cause of obesity 91
   Chew your food 93

6. Daily massages 97
   Daily massage 1: Hair combing 97
   Daily massage 2: Back massage..100
   Daily massage 3: Pericardium meridian massage 103
   Other useful massages 105

7. The future of Traditional Chinese Medicine and its concept of
   self-healing...109
   Body energy measurement...112
   Meridian data 114
   Conclusion 117

Appendix: Technology and Traditional Chinese Medicine............119
   The Meridian Monitoring System..121
   Meridian *Qi* treatment...123

Index   126

ABOUT THE AUTHOR

In the 1990s Alex Wu worked in Shanghai as a fund manager for a group of investors from Hong Kong. After years of heavy workload and high pressure, his health deteriorated and he faced a multitude of illnesses.

At that time he was fortunate to meet a very skillful Traditional Chinese Medicine (TCM) practitioner. With her help he was able to overcome his illnesses and regain his health in a matter of months. His speedy recovery sparked his interest in TCM and he began studying Chinese medicine. In doing so he compiled a summary of what he had learnt that became the first draft of this book.

He now has a health spa in Taipei where he puts TCM-related equipment that he has helped to design into practice – the Meridian Monitoring System and the Meridian Qi Treatment System, described in the Appendix: Technology and Traditional Chinese Medicine (page 119). The spa opened in late 2014 and provides diagnostics and massage treatments including the massage programme described in Chapter 6 and the related Youtube video.

INTRODUCTION

Are you ready to live past 100 years old?

I recently went to a hospital to visit a 93-year-old friend. He was sharing a room with two other patients, aged 90 and 94. I was quite surprised. I recalled that when I was a kid living in Tainan, a city in southern Taiwan, any funeral I attended in my neighbourhood was generally for someone in their 70s. Back then, living past 70 won you praise for longevity, in stark contrast to today when living past 80 or 90 has become common.

Yet is living to such an advanced age really a blessing? When I look around at middle-aged people – my contemporaries – it is rare to find anybody who is not burdened by some form of chronic illness, whether high blood pressure, type-2 diabetes, gout, or arthritis, or even memory loss. The average person in my age group is bound to be plagued by ailments. In fact, according to the Centers for Disease Control and Prevention in the United States, about half of all adults in the US, so some 162 million people, have chronic health conditions, and one out of four adults has two or more. In most cases, their chronic illnesses will only worsen with age and they will be dependent on medication for the rest of their lives. That may mean 40 to 60 years of coping with illness – a frightening thought.

Life expectancy around the world increased dramatically in the 20th century. In 1900 life expectancy for both men and women in the United States – as well as in most developed countries – was around 50 years. By 2014, in the United States it had increased to 77.4 for men and 82.2 for women, and more than 30 countries had life expectancies above 80. Even more extraordinary is that the rate of increase has not slowed significantly in recent years, so we can expect this figure to continue to rise for the foreseeable future. It is quite possible that by the time people now aged under 50 reach their late 80s or 90s, their life expectancy will have increased to well over 90. Living past 100 will no longer be a rare feat. In fact it will become the norm for the wider population. Extreme longevity will no longer be a prized achievement. It will have become inevitable.

With that in mind, maintaining a good quality of life that allows you to enjoy those extra years should be a top priority for everyone. Depending on your health, an extended lifespan could feel like a true extension of your youthful years or, conversely, a gruelling day-to-day grind in which you cling on to life by depending on an assortment of medications.

For example, a person with acute gout may suffer constant pain and immobility. For that particular person, enjoyment of outdoor activities becomes a distant memory. Even everyday activities that used to be effortless become a painful challenge. To take another case, someone who has advanced type-2 diabetes faces strict restrictions on diet, routine tests for blood sugar levels and a complicated regimen of medications, as well as the fear of significant complications. Thus it is important that we develop healthy living habits at a young age so that we can enjoy our extra years and fulfill our life's potential. In the future, when high life expectancy seems inevitable, simply achieving a great age should no longer be the goal.

The current retirement age in most developed countries is around 60 to 65, an age first determined when the average life expectancy in those countries was around 70. The typical person who retired at 65 could expect five years of leisure before dying of old age. That was the vision in most societies of how a person would spend the latter stages of his or her life. So as our life expectancy rises and the extent of our post-retirement time increases, our attitude to retirement needs to change. Of the many aspects of what a fulfilling life in retirement should entail, whether it is having enough money to last through those years or having a loving spouse or partner to spend those years with, the most important factor is health.

When I observe and talk with the many elderly people around me, I notice that those who have attained an advanced age are not necessarily those who have been healthy all through their lives. On the contrary, many have chronic illnesses that were discovered decades ago and for which they have been taking medication ever since. To me this is one of the many accomplishments of modern medicine – the ability of people to live the longest time while carrying the greatest number of illnesses. It is a feat no doubt, but not necessarily one that people should aim for if they strive for quality rather than quantity of life.

To maintain our health and extend our youthful years for as long as possible, it is important for us to educate ourselves in methods that can improve our general health. We should focus more on illness prevention rather than simply using medication to cope with the symptoms once they occur. By learning the right concepts and establishing healthy living methods, it is not at all difficult to slow down aging and prevent chronic diseases from plaguing our lives. This is what this little book sets out to explain.

Traditional Chinese Medicine – the past and present

When I was growing up in Taiwan I found the story of King Midas and his Golden Touch particularly interesting. Midas is popularly remembered for his ability to turn everything he touched into gold. For many centuries, a common goal of researchers was to make this myth into a reality. Alchemy, a study aimed at transforming base metals into gold, was the driving force of scientific endeavour in the Western world throughout the Middle Ages. In the Far East however, the goal of scientific exploration was aimed in a different direction. Rather than wealth, Chinese emperors yearned for eternal youth and life.

The outcome of that pursuit is what we today call Traditional Chinese Medicine (TCM). At the root of TCM is a philosophy that compares the human body to a universe. The Ying Yang theory of opposites and the Five Elements theory (which I explain on page 53) are the governing laws of such a universe. Only in the past century did those ancient Chinese philosophies and theories became known to the Western world, but because they lack a scientific basis they have been deemed 'pseudoscience' by Western and even Chinese societies.

With the blossoming of the internet, basic knowledge of computer science and systems has become common currency among most educated people. When we re-examine the old TCM theories using that knowledge, we can develop a deeper comprehension of them. Put simply, the Ying Yang theory and the Five Elements theory were methods used to describe complex systems at a time when instruments and data were nonexistent.

The central theme of TCM is the use of comparisons between the human body and things that are known in nature. Back in the time when TCM theories were first constructed it was impossible to develop a system so complex that it could be compared to a human body. Thus, the Five Elements theory arose. The relationships between the five elements – wood, fire, earth, metal, water – were considered common sense at the time, so it was easier for people to employ

4

these relationships to understand the human body. With today's wide knowledge of technology and systems, we no longer need to use such primitive methods. TCM theories are understandable using modern-day terminology that is more accessible to the average person. The goal of the *User's Manual for the Human Body* is to make such a link between the present and the past.

After many years of studying TCM, I discovered that the incorrect use of our bodies, which includes incorrect sleeping patterns, incorrect lifestyles, incorrect diet and incorrect responses to diseases, will cause our body energy to decline. Low levels of body energy will result in various chronic diseases. We need energy to stay healthy.

For many years people with chronic diseases have hoped that one day somebody would be able to discover miraculous cures. Such hope is not realistic. On the other hand, by returning to a healthy lifestyle and understanding the basis of good health, we can increase our body energy. Greater body energy ensures better self-healing and self-regenerating capacities, which in turn provide us with the cure for chronic diseases.

Introducing *A User's Manual for the Human Body*

Traditional Chinese Medicine (TCM) has existed in China for thousands of years. Its treatment methods range from a complex herbal system to acupuncture, and a wide variety of massage-related techniques. However, because most TCM theories derive from ancient Chinese writings, they are difficult to translate well enough for foreigners to understand. In fact, it is difficult even for people who are fluent in Chinese to comprehend their full meaning.

My path to studying TCM was rather unusual. In my younger days I worked as a mechanical and computer engineer. I later spent many years as an investment consultant and then as the manager of a multinational company. While my professional career was successful, the tiring nature of my work, as well as the constant high pressure, caused my health to deteriorate. At just 48 years old, I suffered from a multitude of chronic ailments, including rapid hair loss, allergic rhinitis and severe insomnia. While none of these ailments was life-threatening, they greatly affected my quality of life and caused me to fear for my long-term health. I sought help from modern medicine but realised that its treatment methods were aimed at alleviating my symptoms rather than curing my illnesses. I became distraught when handed a prognosis of spending the rest of my life relying on medication. At that time I was fortunate to meet a talented TCM practitioner and massage therapist in Shanghai. Throughout my treatment process, she explained the basic concepts of TCM. The effectiveness of the treatment opened my eyes to the healing potential of TCM for some of the most troubling chronic ailments. I spent many years studying TCM and kept a journal that eventually became the initial draft of this book.

Back in 2002 I completed the Chinese version of *A User's Manual for the Human Body*. I had no plans to publish the book as it was simply a text file in my computer. Many of my close friends knew about my interest in TCM and many of them asked for my opinion regarding their own health issues, mostly chronic illnesses. Instead of having a lengthy discussion every time this occurred, my response was to send them my book and ask them to consider my ideas. Eventually one of my friends asked me whether I would allow them to send it to their friends. Since the reason I had written the book in the first place was to share my ideas with other people, I agreed without hesitation.

I completely forgot that the book was being distributed online, till in 2005, while I was exchanging business cards with a new acquaintance during dinner, the person saw my name on the card and expressed positive surprise. She was the owner of a restaurant and she told me that she was currently reading my book. I was puzzled, because I had never published any books. The only 'book' that I had ever written was still sitting in my computer. She then pulled something out of her handbag and showed it to me. It was a stack of paper organized in a binder. The cover read *A User's Manual for the Human Body*, naming me as its author. When I got home that night, I went online and searched for my name and my book. It was then that I realised it was downloadable from hundreds of Chinese websites. At the end of 2005, online book reviewers hailed my book as one of the most downloaded e-books of the year.

Not long after that I was contacted by several publishers and in mid-2005 and early 2006, my book was published in Taiwan and China. Because of its online popularity, sales figures were high from the start and reached one million copies by the end of 2007, breaking the sales record in China for health-related books. In the past, publishers generally precluded free online distribution of published books for fear of limiting sales, yet this one continues to be available online as it was originally. Its success made it a famous example of unconventional marketing within the publishing industry in China.

After receiving an overwhelmingly positive response from readers in the Chinese community, the Korean edition was released in late 2007 and the Japanese in 2009. By understanding the concepts and practising the methods described in the book, many people have achieved a healthier lifestyle. I am delighted it is appearing in English and German in 2018. I hope that in the near future it will be translated into many more languages, so that even more people can benefit from better health.

氣 血

CHAPTER

1

The point of view of a product designer

When my first book came out in Chinese, several of my friends asked me about the title. The term 'user's manual' is not common for a book that talks about healthy living. However, on my journey studying Traditional Chinese Medicine (TCM) I have found that it looks at the human body in much the same way as a product designer looks at, and explains, a new piece of equipment. I therefore decided that should be the approach and title of my book. Thinking about and analysing the causes of chronic illnesses from the product designer's perspective often yielded new possible causes that could result in solutions that would otherwise have been difficult to discover.

In my early 20s, as I have said, I was a research and development engineer. After completing each new product, a user's manual always needed to be written. Since I was the developer of the product, I was commonly one of the few people who could write the manual. When I first read *The Yellow Emperor's Inner Canon*, one of TCM's oldest and most important texts, I was astonished to find that the structure of the book was very similar to that of a user's manual. It begins by explaining the human body's environment (depending on seasons, temperature, humidity etc) and how we should be living within that environment, in a way that is like a user's manual, explaining how a product should be used. The *Canon* then explains the systems and functions of the human body, just as a manual will outline the specifics of a product. Just as going against the instructions in the user's manual will often lead to a product malfunctioning, it is not new for people to ignore good advice about healthy living. Consequently, a large portion of *The Yellow Emperor's Inner Canon* is dedicated to explaining how to diagnose and treat illnesses after they emerge.

A computer user's manual is usually written by the R&D engineers. As regards its structure and content, *The Yellow Emperor's Inner Canon*, although of course not written by the designer of the human body, was at least written from the perspective of such a person. When we look at modern medicine from that same angle, we see that its diagnoses are built from the ground up through countless repeated observations of symptoms, a form of diagnosis constructed from a user's, not a designer's, perspective. The two vastly different approaches to diagnosing an illness yield completely different treatment philosophies and techniques, as I will describe.

Given my background in R&D engineering, it is second nature for me to view all objects from a designer's perspective, including the human body. Whenever I am faced with illness or discomfort, my first thought is always: 'If I were the designer of this body, how would I have designed it to deal with these problems?'

When we design a computer, maintenance is something that must be taken into consideration. The standard maintenance procedures need to be considered during product design. Without proper maintenance, a computer will not be able to function for long. Modern computers are equipped with an array of self-diagnostics and self-repairing tools that prevent malfunctions. Compared with the average lifespan of computers, the average human body can function for a very long time. Thus it is logical to assume that our body must also carry within it a highly intelligent, superbly functioning self-healing system.

On a philosophical level, modern medicine and TCM's use of the body's self-healing system are quite different. While on the surface it may appear that modern science acknowledges that the body has the ability to heal itself, its prescribed treatment methods seldom make use of the body's self-healing mechanisms. When dealing with illnesses, modern medicine's methods typically assume that either the body's self-healing system is malfunctioning, or that the threat is beyond the healing ability of the body. Following those lines of thinking, we logically arrive at the conclusion that to overcome illnesses we must rely on exterior methods.

TCM on the other hand approaches any illness with the assumption that the human body is highly intelligent and vigorously resistant to malfunctions. When TCM doctors are confronted with an illness, instead of assuming that it is the result of the body's self-healing system having been defeated, the TCM doctor will recognise the possibility that the symptoms are merely the by-product of a functioning self-healing system. While this difference in philosophy may not seem large, the direction of the healing methods that the two philosophies give rise to will end up at the opposite ends of the spectrum. A doctor who believes a patient's body is failing and a doctor who believes a patient's body is still functioning will react differently to any symptom that the patient develops.

Let us imagine that treating a human illness is similar to treating a computer virus. There are typically two methods to choose between. Either we can locate and delete the file manually, or we can activate an anti-virus program which will remove the infected file automatically. The method that modern medicine employs is similar to the former, a method that is both tiresome and wildly inefficient. Viruses enter the system far faster than technicians can eliminate them. The optimal method is to use an anti-virus program that is built into the system. That anti-virus program is equivalent to our body's self-healing system. What we need to do is to ensure that the anti-virus program is functioning properly and allow it to do its job.

Perhaps the designer of the human body has already stored the necessary tools to deal with all kinds of illnesses. According to the philosophy of modern medicine, none of these tools can be used. Doctors are like a bunch of computer technicians who do not use anti-virus programs, instead deploying their limited knowledge to deal with problems that even they do not understand. Maybe that is one of the reasons why there are so many chronic diseases that have no cure. Maybe that is what pushes medical bills through the roof.

If we can find out what useful self-healing 'software' we have stored inside the body, and properly put that to use, the likelihood of finding solutions to illnesses may increase tremendously. So when we are taking care of our health, it is important to understand that the body already has a self-healing system in place, and can deal with most damage and illness on its own. The key here is knowing how to turn on and fortify that system.

The body's self-healing system is very powerful. Not only can it rebalance your organs when they have fallen out of balance, but it can repair and even replace broken parts. It can self-diagnose, distribute and manage energy, and decide on the proper time to fix each and every organ. The only requirement for activating and maintaining this system is sufficient Blood and *Qi* (explained on page 21), along with quality sleep. Most of the body's major healing processes occur during the night as we sleep. The body will have enough energy to repair its organs only when the brain is sleeping.

In the foreseeable future, healthcare methods that assist the self-healing system will appear on the market – methods that connect with and directly boost self-healing. They are almost certain to have the greatest likelihood of success.

Using a product designer's point of view to solve chronic illnesses: a simple example

Gout is an illness that affects roughly 4% of Americans and an estimated one in 40 (2.5%) in the UK. Indeed, the *Daily Mirror* announced 'Britain is the gout capital of Europe' in January 2014 based on a research paper that showed a nearly 64% rise in cases since 1997.*

As with most chronic illnesses, there is currently no cure. The available treatments for gout are aimed at relieving the symptoms of an acute attack. However, the symptoms recur and the condition of the affected area typically worsens over time. Using the logic that has just been discussed, let me explain TCM's approach to gout and how TCM's treatment is superior to that of modern medicine.

First, let us understand what gout is. Uric acid is one of the acids found in our blood. It crystallises when the level rises too high. Gout occurs when crystallised uric acid is deposited in joints and tendons, which leads to swelling of the joints. This is painful and in severe cases it renders patients unable to move their joints. To treat the condition, modern medical treatments are aimed at accomplishing two goals: reducing the inflammation in the affected area and reducing blood uric acid levels to prevent future attacks. While treatments for reducing inflammation are effective, though with a lot of side effects, modern

* Kuo C-F, Grainge MJ, Mallen C, Zhang W, Doherty M. Rising burden of gout in the UK but continuing suboptimal management: a nationwide population study. *Annals of Rheumatic Diseases* 2014; 74(4): http://dx.doi.org/10.1136/annrheumdis-2013-204463 http://ard.bmj.com/content/74/4/661

medicine has thus far not found a way to control blood uric acid levels. Consequently, the patient will typically have recurrent attacks of gout.

TCM's treatment of gout is completely different in its methodology. Adopting the designer's point of view, let us assume that the inflammation associated with gout is part of the body's healing procedure. In other words, the inflammation is the body's method of dealing with the crystallised uric acid deposits. We know that solid material found inside the bloodstream cannot be transported through the body system. We can think of gout as a condition caused by crystallised uric acid deposits being stuck within the joints. The sharp edges of the uric acid crystals damage the muscle tissue near the affected area, which leads to inflammation and pain. For the body to heal the condition, it must remove these uric acid crystals. However, because the crystals cannot be transported through the bloodstream in their solid state, the body must find a way to transform them into something that is transportable by the blood. To do that, the body must surround the crystals with fluid which then dissolves them. An increase in body fluid is the cause of the swelling. Thus, while the swelling may cause discomfort, it is an essential step in the healing process.

The main problem during this healing process is the inflammation. As I have said, it is thought inflammation occurs when the sharp edges of the uric acid crystals damage the muscle tissue near the affected area. To counter this problem, modern medicine uses various anti-inflammatory drugs such as colchicine and corticosteroids, to prevent inflammation. While this treatment is effective in stopping the pain caused by the inflammation, it does not resolve the core of the gout problem – the existence of crystallised uric acid. The patient receives immediate relief from the symptoms upon treatment, but when the body makes further attempts to remove the uric acid crystals, the swelling will recur as part of the body's healing procedure. Meanwhile, because the uric acid

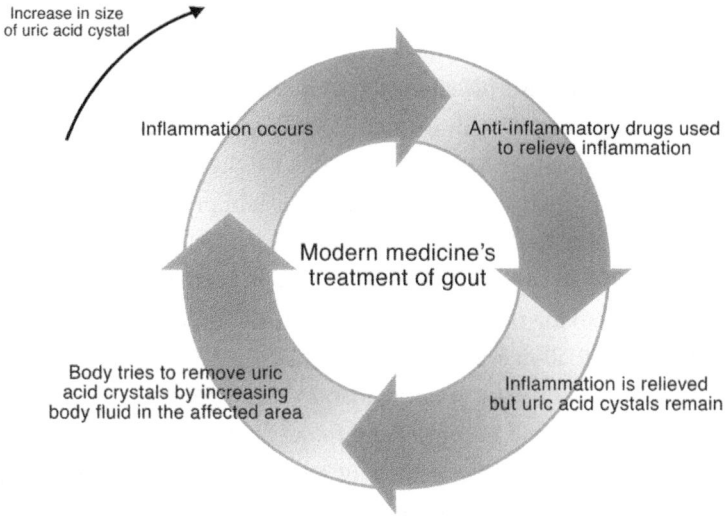

Figure 1.1: Modern medicine's treatment of gout

crystals are never successfully removed, they grow larger and larger as time passes until surgical removal becomes necessary.

Traditional Chinese Medicine's approach to the problem is to view the swelling and inflammation as part of the healing process. Its treatment of gout is not to reduce swelling during gout attacks, but rather to use methods that will strengthen the body's constitution and energy so that the healing process can proceed properly. The patient must limit the movements of the joints that are affected so that further damage does not occur. The swelling and inflammation will stop once the healing process has been completed, which is generally three to five days after the gout attack started. This method, while it puts more stress on the patient during the process, does not lead to the gout becoming worse over time. If the patient can then step away from the poor habits that cause gout to occur, such as lack of sleep, an unhealthy diet and stress, it is possible for the condition to be completely healed by going through this process several times.

The treatment that I have found best for gout using the logic that I described above begins with having the patient increase the intake of antioxidants through either their daily diet or antioxidant nutritional supplements. An increase in antioxidant intake improves the efficiency of the body's self-healing, which in turn *increases* the frequency of gout attacks. Once swelling occurs in the lower body the patient must refrain from walking or any movement that will impact upon the area affected by gout, allow the swelling to subside naturally and continue to maintain a high intake of antioxidants. What will typically happen is that gout attacks will become more frequent but the duration of the swelling will decrease. After each gout attack, the size of the swelling will gradually become smaller until it has completely disappeared.

An important matter to keep in mind is that in order to eliminate the problem, the patient must also make lifestyle and dietary changes. As I have said, in most cases, the cause of gout can be traced back to poor diet, poor sleeping patterns, and/or elevated levels of stress. Therefore, in order to cure the illness completely, one must combine the removal of the current gout with the prevention of future gout.

What is the voltage of the human body?

Computer technology is something that people today are familiar with. As I have said, the logic used in the diagnosic approach of TCM is similar to the approach that a technician uses when servicing a computer. There are many comparisons that can be drawn between a computer and a human body, and I often use the following example to explain how TCM diagnoses and cures diseases.

Every computer has a power supply, used to power the entire computer system. When it fails, the entire system will cease to function. Because of the importance of the power supply, the manufacturer will pay special attention to assuring its durability. Thus, when we take a closer look at the power supply, we can see that allowance is usually made for a fluctuation in external voltage. The reason for this is that in some areas, the voltage coming from an external power source (your wall outlet, for example) may be unstable. To keep the computer running smoothly, the power supply must be able to withstand a certain amount of fluctuation in external voltage. Let us say, for the sake of this example, that the fluctuation range is 35%. For a power supply designed to operate at 110 V, the computer will remain functional, theoretically speaking, when the external voltage drops to 75 V as it is still within the 35% range. If the voltage drops to 65 V, the system will begin to malfunction. If at this point the DVD drive of the computer (to take a slightly outmoded but useful analogy) malfunctions we can deduce that the cause is most likely low voltage and not a malfunction of the DVD drive itself. It is obvious to the computer technician that such a diagnosis depends on prior knowledge that the voltage is not within the acceptable range. If the user or the computer technician has no awareness of the computer voltage, he or she will inevitably come to the conclusion that the problem lies with the DVD drive.

For any computer technician, the first step in the repair of a computer is to check the power supply and voltage. For any hardware-related problem, there exists the possibility that the cause is a lack of power. If a problem with the power supply is fixed, problems associated with a lack of power (for example, a DVD drive malfunction) will be fixed. Now imagine we lack the ability to measure voltage or, worse yet, have no knowledge of voltage. This makes it nearly impossible to carry out proper repairs. Repairs that we undertake without the knowledge of voltage will simply be guesswork.

When we apply the above principles to the human body, we encounter a very significant problem. Which unit of measurement that we are currently using to measure our body is equivalent to the voltage of a power supply? If we consider the voltage of the power supply as the most important measurement for a computer system, is it possible for us to find something of similar importance to a human body? The answer is that there is no such measurement. Modern medicine does not have any method of measuring the voltage of the entire body system, or in simpler terms, the overall health of a person.

We can compare the DVD drive to a body organ – let's say, a kidney. Using the thought process of a computer technician, when a kidney malfunctions, the first step should be to check the voltage of the power supply. However, this is where a huge problem arises. What is the voltage of the human body? Without knowing the voltage, there is no way for us to determine whether anything is wrong with the power supply. Since all we know is that the DVD drive or the kidney is malfunctioning, our only course of action is to repair the kidney. However, no matter how hard we try to repair the kidney, in some cases even going as far as to replace it, we will be unable to fix the problem since the problem did not lie with the kidney to begin with.

In Traditional Chinese Medicine, the voltage of the human body is known as the body energy level. In later parts of this book you will find sections devoted to the concept (see Chapter 2). For now, we can understand body energy as something that is similar to the power supply of a computer. This concept is one of the main differences between TCM and modern medicine.

As I have said, modern medicine has not yet developed a method for measuring body energy. If we compare modern medicine with the field of electronics, we can say that it is still at the stage before the discovery of voltage. Without an understanding of voltage, the field of electronics would not exist. That is exactly why modern medicine finds itself unable to reverse many chronic diseases.

Evidence and proof are the basis of modern medical diagnosis. In the kidney example, since there is no proof of the existence of body energy and since the only evidence present is the malfunctioning of the kidney, the only plausible diagnosis is that the kidney is ailing. Yet for a computer technician, this diagnosis is the equivalent of blaming the DVD drive instead of the power supply. It is hardly surprising that most chronic diseases have no satisfactory remedy.

Just as certain computer parts require a specific amount of power to function, organs require a certain level of body energy to stay healthy. As our body energy level decreases, functions such as self-repair and body-fluid transfer also become sluggish. Many chronic diseases are the direct result of the decline of those functions. By understanding the concept of body energy and how to improve our body energy level, we can find cures for chronic illnesses.

氣 血

CHAPTER
2

Body energy

Body energy is a concept unique to Traditional Chinese Medicine (TCM). The amount of body energy is used as a relative measurement to determine the health of a person. Simply put, a larger amount of body energy indicates that the person is healthier and less prone to diseases and illnesses.

But what exactly is body energy? TCM understands it to be a combination of two elements, **Blood** and *Qi*. Most people find the concept of *Qi* rather mysterious, and indeed it is a topic of great depth and profound theories that go far beyond what I wish to cover in this little book. An analogy I often use when describing *Qi* to those who do not have a deep cultural understanding of the concept is that the body is a battery. Blood is the equivalent of the battery's capacity and *Qi* is the amount of energy currently stored in the battery. It would logically follow that the amount of *Qi* you can have is limited by the capacity of the blood you have. This relationship between Blood and *Qi* is important if we are to understand how to improve our health. Because the quantity of *Qi* a person can have is determined by the storage capacity of Blood they have, the focus of healthy living should be to increase the amount and quality of blood in the body.

TCM asserts that sleep has two very important functions: building Blood and replenishing *Qi*. While the processes pertaining to blood are more or less proven, the replenishment of *Qi* is something that TCM has a model for, but that is difficult to evaluate empirically. The way TCM describes *Qi* is that it is what makes a person energetic. When we wake up in the morning (if we are healthy) we feel refreshed and energised. After working for an entire morning, we start to feel tired in the afternoon. The difference between the state of our body in the morning and the state of our body in the afternoon is a loss of *Qi*. When we rest after feeling tired, our *Qi* is replenished and we feel refreshed.

Blood, on the other hand, is often used in TCM as an indicator of health. The difference between a healthy person and a person who is ill is that a healthy person's body has an abundance of Blood whereas an ill person has a lack of Blood. An abundance of blood means that the person is able to carry more *Qi*, which makes them feel energetic and allows their body to function at its optimal capability.

It is important to remember that when TCM discusses Blood, it is referring to the total quantity of Blood. TCM believes that as our health declines, either due to aging or to other influences, our quantity of blood decreases as well. Since Blood determines how much *Qi* the body can carry, a decrease in its capacity also causes a decrease in available *Qi* for the body to utilise. This means that a person will feel less energetic and be more prone to illnesses, since the body is functioning at a lower level. TCM believes that many chronic diseases are the result of low levels of Blood and *Qi*.

In the following section, I will divide a person's body energy into five levels and discuss in detail how each level affects our bodily functions.

Five levels of body energy

Determining the body energy level of a patient is the most important part of the TCM diagnostic procedure. TCM doctors use various methods of observation to determine this level:

- visual observation of the patient's appearance, including complexion and tongue colour;

- physical observation (touch/palpation) of the patient's pulse and oddities in muscle texture;

- mental observation/consideration of the patient's symptoms and peculiarities.

(Such assessment is, of course, subjective and dependent on the skill of the doctor, but in the Appendix I describe how technology may change this.)

Once the patient's body energy level has been measured, TCM doctors can accurately determine the cause of the illness and formulate an efficient method of treatment.

A person's body energy level can be broken down into five levels. I will now look at each level in detail.

Level 1: Healthy level

This person's body has the optimal level of Blood and *Qi*. Their bodily organs function flawlessly and they do not feel any discomfort. Such a person has a rosy facial complexion and a fit figure. Their body's maintenance tasks are fully up to date and new damage from both interior and exterior causes are dealt with without apparent effort.

From TCM's perspective, this type of person is extremely rare, especially in today's world.

My favourite analogy of energy level is money, or more specifically, a person's lifestyle relative to his or her financial situation. When your earnings are sufficient, you can afford to buy a new car when your old one is well past 200,000 kilometers. A cracked window that could be a safety hazard? You can pay to get it replaced. At this level of super-health, all your faculties are in perfect condition, and you are supremely confident that you have all wear and tear covered.

Level 2: Semi-healthy level

This level of body energy is slightly below level 1. There are many factors that contribute to a decline in body energy. One of the main factors is an unhealthy lifestyle that includes physical strain, such as abnormal sleep patterns and emotional stress. Using the previous financial example, this is when your earnings are insufficient for a luxurious lifestyle. Instead of buying a new car, maybe you buy a seven-year-old used one. You can still get to where you want to go, but that sound you hear when your car comes to a complete stop has you asking questions. In health terms, your body goes through more noticeable maintenance cycles, such as occasional non-infection-related colds (see page 29) and other minor ailments. This is where diagnostic paths first begin to divide. You begin to question whether or not these problems are minor or serious. If you are at the semi-healthy level, the answer is that they are minor, but incorrect treatment could bring the body's energy down to level 3.

Level 3: Sub-healthy level

As body energy continues to decrease, at a certain point the body will reduce the energy spent on maintenance to cope with the demands of staying alive. In financial terms, there are now insufficient funds. Diseases and damage to the bodily organs that pose no immediate threat to the body will be ignored. At this energy level, the body only has enough to maintain daily operations. With a weakened immune system, it no longer engages in unnecessary battles against diseases that are not life-threatening. Despite a lack of symptoms, experienced TCM doctors can detect signs of a decrease in body energy level by observing the patient's appearance.

In today's society, a large proportion of working adults exist at this body energy level. Since these people rarely experience disease symptoms, they are under the false impression that they are in good health.

Using the Blood and *Qi* theory, we can view this energy level (level 3) as indicating that a person is unable to create sufficient Blood. According to TCM theories, Blood is created every night during sleep. A healthy person is able to generate enough blood during sleep to replace that which is used up during the daytime. When the amount used during the day is more than is generated at night, the body will use Blood that is stored inside the liver to cover for this shortfall.

If this shortfall continues, the amount of time the person can maintain their energy level will depend on the amount of Blood that was stored in their younger days. Most people have healthier lifestyles in their youth than when they are adult, though this is changing. The capacity for energy in the body depends on how healthily the person lived when they were young.

Level 4: Energy depletion level

The body's continued use of previously stored Blood depletes these holdings. When the body no longer has enough Blood and *Qi* to maintain its regular functions, the person will feel constant fatigue. At this stage the body will start to break down its muscles in order to generate energy.

People at this energy level are usually in their 50s or 60s. Many of them feel that their health is weakening. However, most are not yet diagnosed with any serious diseases.

Level 5: Complete exhaustion level

At this level, the body has used up most of its available energy. As the organs deteriorate, such a person develops serious diseases, such as cancers, kidney failure, stroke, etc. Since the low energy level affects all the body's organs, the patient will likely develop serious illnesses in multiple organs. Modern medicine may view such phenomena as the spreading of cancer from one organ to another. In TCM's view, such phenomena are due to the deterioration of multiple organs caused by a lack of body energy.

From studying the five levels of body energy, we can see that it is important to determine the cause of the occurrence of symptoms in relation to the person's body energy level.

Using the body energy model, we can see that most disease symptoms occur at two levels: the semi-healthy and the energy depletion levels. (Let us omit the most serious diseases for now as they mostly occur at level 5 – complete exhaustion.) The causes of the symptoms, however, are completely different at each stage. At level 2 (semi-healthy), a person's high energy allows their body to battle constantly against diseases, resulting in frequent symptoms. At level 4 (energy depletion), the person's low body energy level is the cause of the symptoms. Low body energy causes the body to lose some of its proper functions as well as reducing the strength of the immune system. The person will feel constant fatigue, as well as any symptoms associated with the diseases they may contract owing to a weak immune system. Thus, at level 4, while the person may also feel ill, the degree of severity is much greater than that which is encountered at level 2.

As the causes of the symptoms are different for levels 2 and 4, the treatment methods used are also different.

At level 2, as we have seen, the symptoms are the result of the body's counter measures against diseases. TCM views these symptoms as among the body's proper functions, which means that they should not be treated as illnesses. We should instead allow the body to perform its functions while aiding it by providing proper rest and nutrition. This method is in stark contrast to the conventional method of treating symptoms to stop them from occurring.

At level 4, the cause of the symptoms is much more serious. Given the depleting energy level, the body is unable to function properly. Coupled with a weakened immune system, one of the bodily functions that is underperforming, the person will experience a variety of symptoms resulting from both internal body weakening and external diseases. TCM's treatment for this scenario is much more complex. A person with body energy depletion must alleviate symptoms that are life-threatening or that prevent the person from increasing body energy, specifically symptoms that deprive the person of proper sleep and nutrition. Once these symptoms have been dealt with, the focus of the treatment will be to increase the person's body energy to a healthier level.

Figure 2.1 (page 28) illustrates the five levels of body energy. An encouraging point that we should keep in mind is that the decrease in body energy is a slow process. Depending on a person's constitution, those with an unhealthy lifestyle can spend years or even decades at the sub-healthy level before reaching the energy depletion level. In contrast to the decrease in body energy, an increase in body energy takes much less time. Once a person switches from an unhealthy lifestyle to a healthy one, they can experience positive changes in a matter of months. We can compare our body to a common smartphone battery. A fully charged smartphone can be used for hours or even days yet once the battery is depleted, it requires only a fraction of time for recharging. The human body is even more efficient.

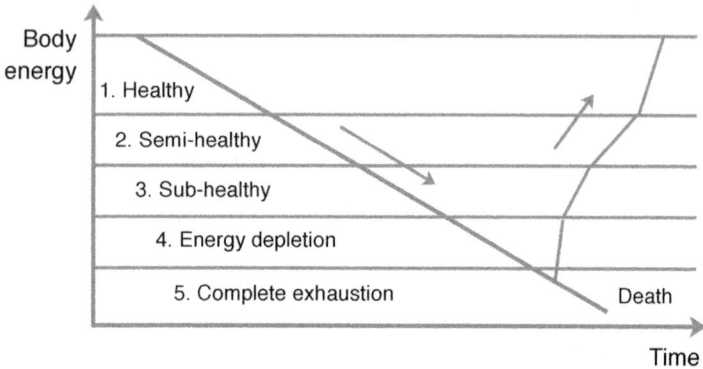

Figure 2.1: The five levels of body energy

With Figure 2.1 in mind, the concept of healthy living becomes apparent, though it is rather abstract compared with the concept of body energy. Just how healthy are you? Are you healthier than you were two months ago? How about a year ago? Not only are there no methods of measuring health, there are no ways of actually describing it.

Based on the five levels of body energy, we can have an understanding of how healthy a person is in terms of where they are on the body energy chart (Figure 2.1). The goal of healthy living becomes a straightforward one as well: to go from a downward drop to an upward climb on the body energy chart. Many chronic diseases that occur at levels 4 and 5 will not occur at level 3 and above. Increasing body energy allows many chronic diseases to be treated successfully by our own body's self-healing system.

The common cold and TCM's theory of cold-temperature damage

The common cold, as its name suggests, is one of the most common diseases that we encounter. Almost every person has experienced the symptoms. Understanding of the common cold is drastically different in modern medicine compared with TCM. These differences in understanding mean that the subsequent treatment is also quite different. TCM asserts that the continuous mistreatment of the common cold by modern medicine directly contributes to the development of several chronic diseases. Let us first examine the differences between modern medicine and TCM in relation to how the common cold is understood.

Modern medicine asserts that the common cold is a viral infectious disease that mainly affects the upper respiratory tract. The symptoms are caused by the body's immune system reacting to the infection. Currently there is no cure for the common cold. All treatments are aimed at reducing the symptoms caused by the cold virus.

Traditional Chinese Medicine on the other hand has a different view. It categorises the common cold into two distinctive types. The first type is similar to modern medicine's understanding that the symptoms are caused by an external pathogen – for example, the cold virus. The second type occurs when the body is in the process of removing 'cold-temperature damage'. TCM views the majority of cold symptoms as of the latter category. While modern medicine is successful at treating the first type, its mistreatment of the second type is the source of many chronic diseases that have their roots in the common cold.

Human body temperature is maintained near a constant level of about 37 degrees Celsius. When the body temperature drops below 35 degrees, the body begins to malfunction. This condition is known as hypothermia, and if left untreated can be fatal. To avoid hypothermia and to maintain body temperature, our body has a mechanism that is activated in response to coldness. TCM's theory of cold temperature damage refers to the byproduct of this mechanism.

When our body encounters a cold temperature, far below our body temperature, our body surface temperature drops, as heat transfers from high temperature areas to low temperature areas. To counter that drop in body temperature, chemical reactions within our body fluid occur, generating heat and raising body temperature back to its normal range. After heat energy has been released, waste material is produced that the body then stores below the skin surface. If the body

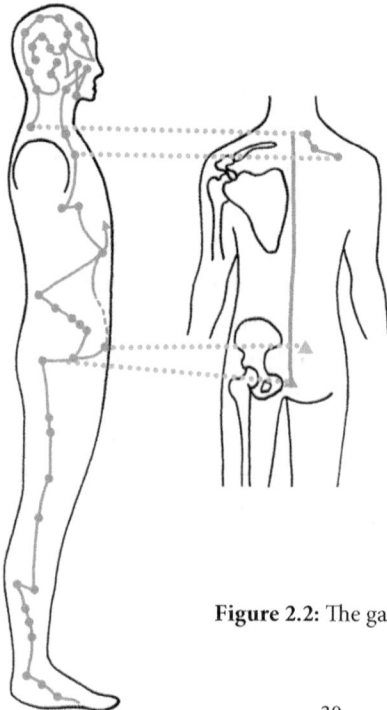

Figure 2.2: The gallbladder meridian

is exposed to cold for a short period of time, it will be able to remove the waste material through its normal metabolism. However, if the body is exposed to cold for a long period of time, the waste material will be transported to the inner parts of the body and stored there while the body surface continues the process of burning body fluid to counter cold temperatures. As more and more waste material builds up inside the body, some of it will travel through the meridians into various body organs (for a discussion of the meridians, see Chapter 3). Over time those waste materials reduce the functionality of the organs as well as lowering the fluidity of the corresponding meridians. Depending on the part of the body that it is exposed to cold, the meridian that is affected and the resulting symptoms vary.

There are many different ways for a person to sustain cold temperature damage (also known as *cold Qi*). The most common of these ways are damage to the gallbladder, stomach and lung meridians. Damage to the gallbladder meridian occurs most frequently. When we look at this meridian in Figure 2.2, we can see that it is thought to extend for quite a long distance and the section that is most vulnerable to cold temperature damage is along the outer thighs. As they are less sensitive to temperature change compared with other areas of the body, people tend to wear less clothing to cover them. For example, while people put on extra clothing to keep their upper body warm, a jacket for example, only when the temperature drops significantly do they put on an extra layer on their legs. For women who wear skirts even in cold weather, the likelihood of sustaining cold temperature damage is even greater. There are several signs that a person may show when they have sustained cold-temperature damage to the gallbladder meridian. Prolonged exposure to cold in the outer thighs will cause these areas to build up an abnormally large amount of fat. Decreased fluidity of the gallbladder meridian will also affect the body's ability to absorb nutrients.

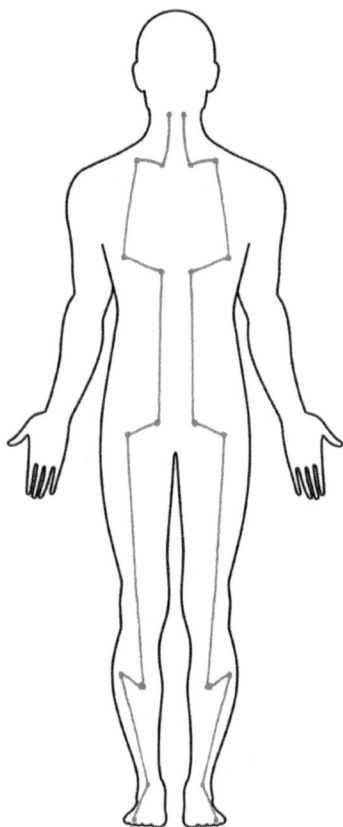

Figure 2.3: The stomach meridian   **Figure 2.4:** The lung meridian

The stomach meridian (Figure 2.3) is commonly affected by cold-temperature damage as well. The source of the damage is primarily our diet. The frequent consumption of cold foods and especially of low-temperature beverages are two of the most common causes of cold-temperature damage to the stomach. A person who has sustained this damage will often suffer from indigestion, frequent attacks of nausea and abdominal bloating.

Compared with the previous two meridians, cold damage to the lung meridian (Figure 2.4) occurs much more rarely. As I will explain later, the 12 meridians can be categorised as either 'Zang' or 'Fu'. The gallbladder and the stomach meridians are Fu meridians, which are less important than the lung meridian, which is a Zang meridian. Cold temperature damage usually occurs within the Fu meridians, but if the body is unable to repair this damage, over time it will infiltrate the body and affect the more important Zang meridians. The lung meridian is the first Zang meridian to be affected by prolonged cold-temperature damage. The resulting symptoms can vary greatly because a person who shows signs of cold-temperature damage in the lungs will also suffer from low body energy. Generally speaking, a well-trained TCM doctor can identify such a person by examining their complexion and their pulse.

The removal of cold-temperature damage and the common cold

As you may have noticed, the symptoms of cold-temperature damage described above do not include the common cold symptoms that people often associate with catching a cold. This is an important distinction that we should keep in mind when trying to understand how TCM views cold symptoms. It sees them as the result of the body *removing* cold-temperature damage, not of its receiving it. A body is only capable of removing cold-temperature damage when it has enough energy. So long as a person's body has a low energy level, while it may have sustained cold-temperature damage, it will not commence the process of repair. Cold symptoms may then not occur even when the body has a large amount of cold-temperature damage.

According to this view, a healthy person, or a person with a high energy level, will frequently experience common cold symptoms. The person's body is able to react quickly to cold-temperature damage by repairing the damage soon after it occurs. Conversely, an unhealthy person or a person with a low body energy level rarely experiences common cold symptoms. The body is weak and unable to get rid of the cold-temperature damage. This view of a person's health contrasts with the way we typically define a healthy person. When we encounter someone who is rarely ill and rarely experiences common cold symptoms, we often view such a person as strong and healthy. However, more often than not the lack of common cold symptoms is due to low body energy rather than high body energy. The body simply lacks the ability to deal with the damage through inflammation.

When one understands that common cold symptoms are caused by the body's removal of cold-temperature damage, it is easy to see how modern medicine mistreats the common cold. If we assume that the symptoms are a necessary part of the body's healing process, using methods that interrupt such a process is actually harmful to the body as it halts the healing process rather than assisting it. People who frequently use cold medicine to stop cold symptoms may be the ones who sustain the most cold-temperature damage. By using cold medicine to stop the symptoms, we stop the body from properly repairing cold temperature damage. The result is that this damage remains in the body and accumulates over time. This leads to a decrease in the fluidity of the meridians and a decrease in the efficiency of the organs. In extreme and prolonged cases, this may lead to chronic diseases or worse.

The most common chronic disease that results from this practice is chronic allergic rhinitis. A person with allergic rhinitis is typically someone who has a moderate to high level of body energy. When such a person has cold-temperature-damage, their body will attempt to remove the damage which causes common cold symptoms. When the person experiences such symptoms, cold medicine is immediately used to halt the symptoms thus preventing the removal process from achieving completion, leaving cold-temperature damage inside the body. However, because the person has enough body energy, the body will attempt to remove the leftover damage at the next opportunity. The result is that the person will frequently experience cold symptoms which are then diagnosed as allergic rhinitis.

TCM's treatment of the common cold is focused on helping the body cope with the symptoms. In some cases, TCM doctors will prescribe herbs that intensify the symptoms, with the goal of shortening the duration of the cold-temperature damage removal process, much like the old-fashioned advice in the UK to 'take Beecham's powders and sweat it out'. Instead of using cold medicine to halt the symptoms, TCM focuses on rest and relies on the body's own self-healing system to carry out its proper functions.

Uncomfortable symptoms may not be diseases

Modern medicine is built upon the assumption that the body easily makes mistakes. Whenever our body displays abnormalities or uncomfortable symptoms, we simply accept that it is the body making a mistake, that we are ill. Because this way of thinking is propagated by education, a perceived link between discomfort and the body being sick has become deeply rooted in our instincts.

Modern medicine recognises in theory that there is a self-healing system, yet in actual diagnostics the self-healing system is treated as almost non-existent. The two facts below help to illustrate this point:

- When uncomfortable symptoms are diagnosed by a doctor, the diagnosis never contains the line: 'Your body is undergoing maintenance on a particular organ'. Instead, the line is: 'There is a problem with a particular organ'. In other words, modern medicine's standard logic says discomfort or abnormality in an organ is an illness.

- With all examination parameters, there is always a normal range. If your test numbers fall outside that range, they are defined as abnormal, and the abnormality is in turn defined as an illness. Never have abnormalities in testing been defined as signs that the body is repairing organs.

From these two facts we can conclude that while modern medicine does not deny that the body has a self-healing system, it believes that when the body repairs its organs there will be no uncomfortable symptoms and that test parameters will not show any abnormality.

In reality, when we have a cut to our skin, we experience symptoms such as swelling, pain, itch, and the formation of scabs. Simple logic leads us to conclude that these are just symptoms of the body repairing the cut. The cut is the illness. The swelling, pain, itch, and formation of scab are symptoms of the body's healing system working as intended. The falling off of the scab at the end is just the loss of waste material created by this process. In the process of healing the cut, all the doctor does is apply anti-inflammatory medicine and disinfectant to the cut. All the repair and regrowth work is handled by the body's own strong self-healing capabilities. In the same way, the body's organs also display powerful self-healing abilities.

The earlier case study of gout is a good example of the body's self-healing system at work. The body's activation of its self-healing mechanisms to remove uric acid crystals causes the patient's painful swelling around the areas where the crystals occur. While those symptoms cause severe discomfort they should not be classified as illnesses. Just like the process of healing a cut to the skin, they are simply evidence of a properly functioning self-healing system.

As I have said, similarly, the body's inner organs have self-healing capabilities. In the course of a maintenance cycle, the body may experience a period of discomfort, along with the creation of waste materials. Waste material close to the skin layer can exit by passing through the skin and directly leaving the body. Waste material deeper in the body is not as simple to deal with. The regular, or expected, flow of waste materials naturally follows normal exit procedures. It is when extra waste needs to be transported that additional pathways are required. As we do not normally use those waste transportation methods, when they are activated we classify that fact as an abnormality, which usually leads to test parameters falling outside the normal range. This is often accompanied by discomfort, leading most people to go to their doctor for blood and urine testing. Undesirable results can arise, prompting the diagnosis that the person is sick. But the additional waste material in the blood and urine that pushed the reading beyond the normal range may have come about because of the body's own maintenance procedures. The abnormalities detected in blood and urine samples may not be signs of illness. They may in fact be the opposite. Such readings may suggest that the body's self-healing system is hard at work fixing the problem, setting the body's condition on an upward course.

There are many cases like this. For example, a common problem in modern-day society is the popularity of 'working hard and playing hard'. There have been many people who, after making improvements to their lifestyles, have started to experience symptoms that can include frequent colds, proteinuria (excess protein in the urine), palpitations, irregular heartbeat, insomnia, headaches, muscle aches and dermatitis. In some cases, if the person happens to undergo a health check-up during such a period, test results may show unexpected increases in blood lipids, blood sugar and cholesterol. All of the above symptoms, even if only occurring temporarily, could be signs of the body performing its self-healing procedures. However, current testing systems categorise all abnormalities as illnesses, so self-healing itself is treated as the enemy. In this situation, we have to consider the following serious problems:

- How many medical procedures are fighting the self-healing process, rather than the actual problem? When we are sick, is modern medicine providing us with positive assistance, or negative interference?

- When the body's maintenance cycles are interrupted, what kind of negative effects are created? Will such interruption create bigger problems for the patient and waste medical resources?

- How many severe diseases are caused by long periods of fighting against our own self-healing system?

- Modern medicine may have serious issues even when it comes to defining diseases.

The situation in which you properly nurse your health in the right direction and your body starts to experience uncomfortable symptoms is well known. These have been labelled 'healing reactions', but most may be symptoms caused by the self-healing system.

In management, there are two main principles guiding the way we act. The first is to 'do the right thing'. The second is to 'do the thing well'. The correct approach to doing work is first to ensure that you're doing the right thing. That is, that the direction in which you are headed is correct. Only then should you proceed to do the thing well. For a long time now, within the medical system, far too many people have been neglecting to 'do the right thing'. Most people just focus on doing the thing well. Many have spent their entire lives specialising in particular medical projects, when, perhaps from the beginning, their direction was off and they're only doing the wrong thing well.

TCM has a famous saying: 'cure the disease, not the symptoms'. When the body shows uncomfortable symptoms, the doctor must use methods of deduction to follow the body's logic in order to find the source of the problem. The goal of treatment should be to deal with the root of the illness, not the symptoms.

If doctors do not use deductive methods and focus solely on the removal of symptoms, it can happen that procedures used to do that cause even greater harm to the body. Dealing with the root cause of the illness is 'doing the right thing'. If you use the wrong methods to deal with the symptoms, even if you really remove the symptoms, oftentimes you are only redirecting the illness deeper into the body. This is 'doing the wrong thing well'.

Let us take the common cold as an example, as before. The term 'catching a cold' is used in English. It suggests that something cold enters the body. This cold object is called '*cold Qi*' in TCM terminology (see page 31). When *cold Qi* first enters the body, it stops at the body's outer layers. At this stage, it can be removed if we ingest foods or medicines that help the body generate heat. The real cause of the common cold is that *cold Qi* enters the body, so the focus should be on helping the body remove it, rather than stopping the symptoms of a cold.

Sneezing and a runny nose are ways by which the body removes water through the nasal passages. TCM deems that the body uses the exiting water to transmit *cold-Qi*-carrying bodily fluid. Water is like the cooling agent (freon) in air conditioning. Normally, you do not sneeze or have a runny nose. When these symptoms arise, the body is not used to them, so naturally they feel uncomfortable.

If we treat sneezing and a runny nose as a problem that requires treatment and apply medicine to stop these symptoms, we end up halting the body's *cold-Qi*-removing process, which forces the *cold Qi* to remain in the body and, over time, moving deeper, it eventually enters the lungs and causes far greater problems.

In the example of gout, as I described earlier, swelling is in fact the body's attempt to dissolve uric acid crystals that accumulate in the joints by surrounding them with body fluid. Doing the wrong thing well would be to use medication to disrupt the swelling. The symptoms have been erased but so has the energy invested by the body in solving the problem. Maintenance, though we often take it for granted, can tax the body. It can only occur when your body energy is above a certain level, because energy needs to be expended to conduct it. When you forcefully cancel the self-healing system's efforts, it has to save up that energy again so that it can perform the same act twice, or three times, or even more.

Doing the wrong thing well, in this case in particular, is extremely detrimental to the body's health. When the body performs the maintenance procedure of surrounding uric acid crystals with body fluid, the level of healthiness is at a point where the body can carry out this procedure. After medication has been used to reduce swelling, the body may or may not still be above the health level threshold that enables it to perform the act again. If the body can restart the procedure, it will once again use up a large quantity of its resources. If medication is used over and over again, the body will eventually be incapable of restarting maintenance. This puts your health level in a loop, where all your efforts to improve your health will eventually be cancelled out by your body wasting energy on a procedure that it must perform, yet is prevented by medication from doing so.

Throughout this book, I will point out further examples parallel to that of gout that demonstrate a glaring need to differentiate between actual diseases and symptoms of bodily maintenance. Correctly understood, maintenance symptoms are easily handled and are generally not serious health risks. But when handled incorrectly they will gradually wear your self-healing system down.

How to increase body energy, and the importance of sleeping early

Whenever I am asked about the key to improving health, my answer always focuses on the improvement of body energy, or 'Blood and *Qi*'. I have described the varying levels of body energy and how each level relates to the health of an individual. The goal of healthy living under the philosophies of TCM is to move upwards in energy level. But how can that be done?

To summarise in brief the relationship described between Blood and *Qi*: Blood is the storage capacitor for *Qi*. The maximum amount of *Qi* that the body can carry depends on the total amount of Blood. If the goal is to increase the total amount of Blood and *Qi*, then the focus of our lifestyle should be on increasing the body's total Blood quantity.

There are two main factors that affect our body's Blood production. The first is the absorption of nutrients. We can think of nutrients as the raw materials that the body uses for Blood production. The second factor is sleep, during which the nutrients are processed into Blood. Both factors are equally important to blood production and a deficiency in either area will result in low production, which over time will result in low Blood and *Qi* levels, or low body energy.

In ancient China, around the time that most Traditional Chinese Medicine theories were formulated, food was less abundant than in modern times. Malnutrition was common. In classic TCM texts, many of the illnesses that were caused by low blood and *Qi* were typically related to the lack of nutrition. In modern times, however, food shortage is generally not a problem in most developed countries. When we encounter people who have low body energy due to malnutrition, the cause is probably low nutrient absorption rather than a lack of food. Massaging the gallbladder meridian and properly chewing your food are two topics that will be discussed later on in the book. Properly chewing your food and maintaining the fluidity of your gallbladder meridian will greatly improve your nutrient absorption.

The second factor that hinders Blood production is a lack of sleep. Similar to nutrient absorption, a lack of sleep has become much more common in modern times. The classic TCM text *The Yellow Emperor's Inner Canon* recommended that people go to sleep early during winter time and late during the summer. It is interesting to note that the text's idea of sleeping early refers to 7-8 pm and sleeping late to 9-10 pm. By today's standards, anyone who sleeps before midnight may be considered an early sleeper. With this in mind, it is not difficult to determine that for many people a lack of sleep is most probably the main contributing factor to low body energy.

The human body has an optimal period for Blood production. The best time is from 9 pm to about 1 am, with a slight variation depending on the time of dusk and dawn at your location. If a person can achieve deep sleep during this period, he or she will provide the body with the optimal conditions for generating blood and increasing body energy. For people who want to maintain a healthy level of body energy, I suggest going to sleep no later than 10 pm. If a person can achieve deep sleep in one hour after falling asleep, sleeping at 10 will give the person two hours of optimal Blood production. For the average person, I suggest at least eight hours of optimal Blood production per week. For those who are ill or have low body energy, more time would be beneficial to their recovery.

A question I am often asked is whether or not a person can sleep beneficially during the day instead of at night. For example, a person working the late-night shift may sleep from 8 am until 4 pm. While that person is still getting eight hours of sleep, blood production is quite different. The human body has a biological clock that governs the various processes that take place in it throughout the day. In TCM, the theory of Midnight-Moon Ebb-flow (*Zi Wu Liu Zhu*) describes how the body functions in the daytime. For anyone interested in learning TCM theory or doing any form of meditation, I strongly recommend studying this theory as it describes in detail how *Qi* travels across meridians. To keep things simple in this introductory book, we can consider the theory to be a time schedule for the 12 meridians. The liver and gallbladder meridians, which govern Blood production, are only active during nighttime, thus it is incumbent upon us to achieve deep sleep during those hours to maximise this.

Aside from these two main factors, other variables may affect the body's Blood production. They may be internal, such as stress or depression, or external, such as environmental pollution, but generally speaking, sleep deficiency and poor nutrient absorption cover the majority of cases in which a person suffers from low body energy. If we can make sure that we give our body enough fuel and time for Blood production, we can increase our body energy over time and improve our health.

氣 血

CHAPTER
3

Traditional Chinese Medicine's understanding of how the human body functions

Before discussing the self-healing system in more detail, it is important to explain Traditional Chinese Medicine's (TCM's) concept of how the human body works. TCM views the entire body as a complete system and the organs as all closely linked with one another. None of the organs works in isolation, and they are never viewed in isolation in Chinese diagnostics. Indeed, the TCM diagnostic approach is based upon the various ways in which organs influence one another.

The human body has far too many organs for each and every one, and their relations with one another, to be analysed individually. A way to illustrate this problem is to imagine that your body consists only of your heart and eyes. The number of links you can draw between your organs is just one. If then you have lungs as well, there would be a link between the heart and the lungs, the lungs and the eyes, and the heart and the eyes: a total of three links. As we add the brain, ears, nose, mouth, hands, feet, skin, hair, large intestine, small intestine, and so on, the number of links increases exponentially (see Figure 3.1) and becomes impossible to analyse.

Qigong is a meditation technique that has existed in China for thousands of years. The main purpose of the practice is to cultivate and channel *Qi* (energy). Practitioners of *Qigong* long ago discovered that *Qi* flows along particular paths inside the human body, known as **meridians**. *Qi* is energy that the body is equipped with from birth. While TCM practitioners are trained to measure *Qi,* modern technology is even now incapable of detecting it. However, as I describe in the Appendix (page 121), equipment has been developed that can detect *Qi* and measure its fluctuations in real time. It is possible that in the near future, these technologies could be used to prove the existence of *Qi* at a scientific level.

Qigong practitioners charted these *Qi* flows and created the meridian charts that exist today. In South America, back in ancient times, the Incan shamans made a similar chart. The two civilisations were in opposite parts of the world, tens of thousands of miles apart, yet they created charts that were almost identical.

Through a long period of experimentation, the individual meridian points were categorised into sections (meridian lines), with each section linked to the corresponding organ(s) that it influenced. The 14 resulting main meridians include 12 paired meridians and two single meridians. The 12 paired meridians correspond to 12 different organs, with the two single meridians being the front and back centre lines of the body from top to bottom (called the Governing Vessel and the Conception Vessel).

Qigong practitioners also found a strong correlation between discomforts in particular organs and the clogging of flow in their respective meridians. Using certain *Qigong* techniques, the meridians could be unclogged by focusing on the affected meridian points, and this in turn resolved the discomfort in the corresponding organs.

From a design perspective, meridians can be viewed as pathways for bodily maintenance. When the body's organs are not functioning optimally, signals are sent from the meridian points, causing pain. Our instinctive reaction when the signal reaches the brain is to rub or lightly tap the meridian point that is hurting. This helps to unclog the meridian point, improving the functioning of the corresponding organ in the process.

Not all organs have corresponding meridian points. This leads to the important categorisation of organs with and organs without meridian points. Organs with meridian points are those that need to be directly treated, whereas organs without meridian points do not. When an organ without any meridian points malfunctions, the malfunction may not arise from that organ itself. The real cause of the discomfort may lie in the 12 organs with meridians. It is these that should therefore be treated.

For example, the skin has no corresponding meridian. Dry skin can cause a variety of discomforts and illnesses. TCM believes the primary cause of dry skin lies in the body's inability to distribute water efficiently to the entire body. Therefore, the lungs, which are responsible for water distribution, are likely to be the cause of the discomfort or illness. To cure problems of the skin, the lungs need to be treated first.

System simplification

The first step to system simplification reduces all the body's organs to 12 meridians, as I have described. The second step is to observe the relationships between the 12 meridians: the heart, small intestine, liver, gallbladder, spleen, stomach, lungs, large intestine, kidney, bladder, pericardium, and *Sanjiao* (thoracic cavity). As I have said, TCM views the human body as a complete system; there are close ties between each organ. In other words, the entire body system can be simplified into 12 sub-systems – the 12 main meridians. By understanding the relationship between them, we can construct a system of logic for how the body communicates and deals with illnesses, as well as finding solutions and treatments for those illnesses.

Figure 3.1 illustrates the 12 main meridians, and the 66 links that can be drawn between them. Understanding all 66 is a tedious and difficult task, so to be useful the system must be further simplified.

By examining the location of the meridians, we can see that there are six that travel along the arms (heart, small intestine, lungs, large intestine, pericardium, and *Sanjiao* (thoracic cavity)) and six that travel along the legs (liver, gallbladder, spleen, stomach, kidney and bladder). Out of the six meridians that travel along the arms, we can see that three

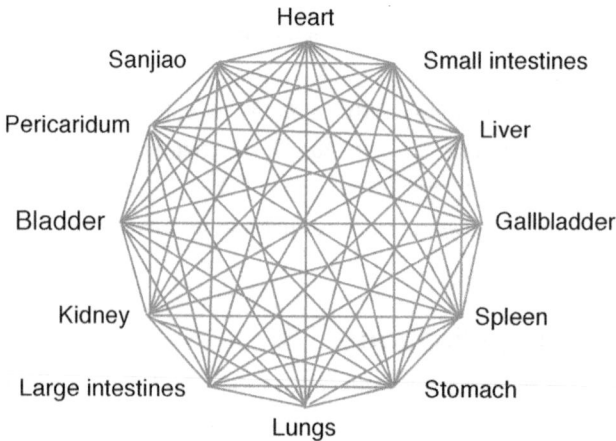

Figure 3.1: The 66 relationships between the 12 meridians

travel along the inner side of the arms and three along the outer. The locations of the inner and outer meridians correspond to one another, forming three pairs of meridians: those for the heart and small intestine, lungs and large intestine, pericardium and *Sanjiao* (thoracic cavity). The same pairings can be made for the meridians that travel along the legs: liver and gallbladder, kidney and bladder, spleen and stomach.

The pericardium and *Sanjiao* meridians are in charge of the body's Blood and *Qi*, respectively. The pericardium influences Blood flow, while the thoracic cavity (*Sanjiao*) meridian influences the flow of *Qi*. These two meridians are considered to make up the body's energy control system, and they can be looked at separately from the other main meridian sub-systems for now. That leaves 10 sub-systems.

Figure 3.2 (a) shows the palm-side view of the left arm. It contains the heart, lung and pericardium meridians. The lung meridian reflects the lungs, and is closely tied to their performance. Massaging the lung meridian can improve the performance of the lungs. Likewise, the heart and pericardium meridians influence the performance of their respective organs. Massaging them can also have a positive effect. The right arm and hand have the same set of meridians. The arms have identical sets of six meridians, while the legs have the remaining, and

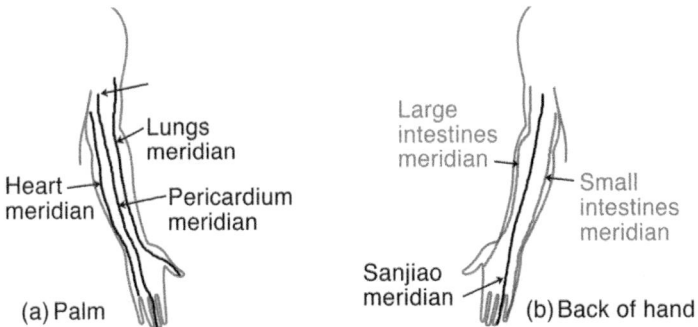

Figure 3.2: The meridians in the arms – (a) heart, lung and pericardium meridians; (b) large intestine, small intestine and *Sanjiao* meridians

again identical, sets of six meridians. The left and right sides of the body have symmetric meridian structures.

Figure 3.2(b) shows the backhand view of the left arm. It contains the small intestine, large intestine and *Sanjiao* meridians. As with the three on the palm-side, the small and large intestine meridians influence their respective organs. Massaging them improves their respective performance. The *Sanjiao* meridian influences the thoracic cavity, and when massaged, improves the flow of *Qi* in the chest area. This is often used to relieve discomfort in the torso.

Figure 3.3 shows three cross-sections through the arm. From the first (a) we can see that when acupuncture needles are inserted into the heart and small intestine meridians, the tips of the needles are very close together. The second cross-section (b) shows how the pericardium

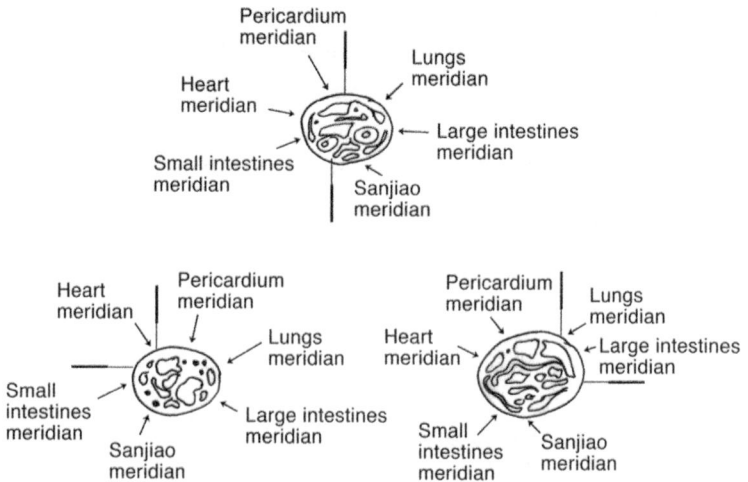

Figure 3.3: Cross sections through the arm showing the relative positions of the acupuncture sites: (a) heart and small intestine; (b) pericardium and *Sanjiao*; (c) lungs and large intestine.

and *Sanjiao* meridians correspond. The third (c) concerns the lung and large intestine meridians.

We should note that these pairings have great importance in TCM diagnostics. As people have discovered over time through extensive clinical experience, illnesses that affect one meridian will have direct influence on the meridian with which it is paired. An example of this would be a patient suffering from the common cold. In TCM, the common cold is described as cold energy attacking the lung system. During a cold, patients will often experience constipation or diarrhoea, demonstrating how the lungs and large intestine influence one another.

Further useful simplification can then be made by using the concepts of *Zang* and *Fu* which categorise the 10 body sub-systems. An interesting observation about *Zang* and *Fu* concerns the physical makeup of the organs to which they relate. All of the organs designated as *Zang* have a complex internal structures: the heart, liver, kidneys, spleen, lungs, and pericardium. The organs designated as *Fu*, on the

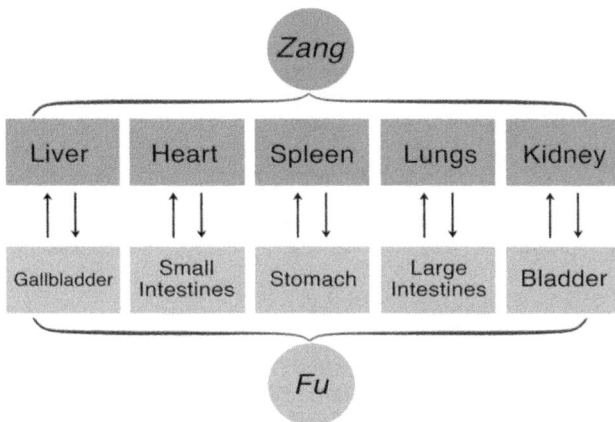

Figure 3.4: The 10 body sub-systems (aside from the pericardium and *Sanjiao*) designated *Zang* or *Fu* and how these interrelate.

other hand, have a hollow interior: the small intestine, gallbladder, bladder, stomach, large intestine, and *Sanjiao* (thoracic cavity).

When the 10 sub-systems are split into *Zang* and *Fu*, we are left with five *Zang* and five *Fu*. Each *Zang* organ fluctuates together with its corresponding *Fu* organ, and the two together can be viewed as one sub-system. In this way, 10 sub-systems are simplified down to five. The 66 system links are thus reduced to only five (see Figure 3.4), facilitating the use of the traditional Five Elements (wood, fire, earth, metal and water) Theory diagnosis.

To recap, starting with numerous organs, TCM simplifies them into 12 main meridians. Pairing the five *Zang* and five *Fu* meridians, while keeping the two meridians for Blood and Qi separate (as these are not systems or organs per se), reduces those to five sub-systems. The

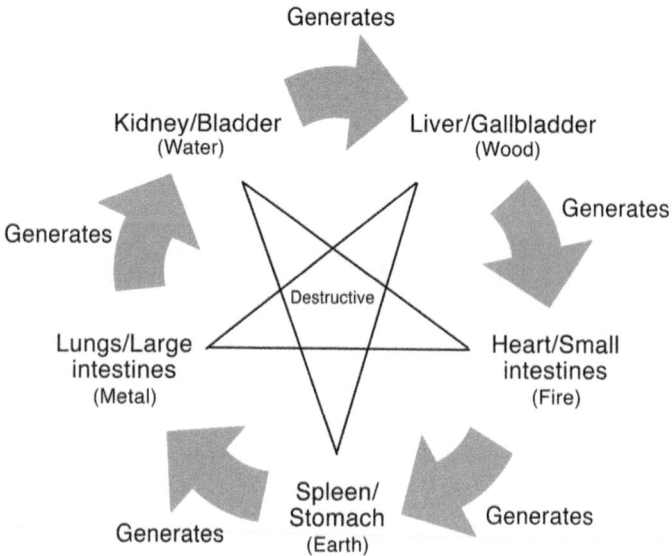

Figure 3.5: How the five sub-systems and the elements to which they relate affect one another positively (arrows) and negatively (star).

relationships between the five sub-systems can then be summarised as shown in Figure 3.5.

Traditionally each sub-system has been associated with one of the **five elements** which relate the state of the human body to the natural environment: liver–gallbladder with wood; heart–small intestines with fire; spleen–stomach with earth; lung–large intestines with metal; kidney–bladder with water. (It is important to note that it is not the five elements themselves that are significant – they were used in ancient times as a memorisation tool that related to known entities; it is the relationships between the organs that have been observed over time and thereby organised into a system that are important.) When a negative effect occurs in one of the elements, it will cause a negative effect in a corresponding element. Wood will affect earth, earth will affect water, water will affect fire, fire will affect metal, metal will affect wood, which will affect earth, and so the cycle continues. For example, when a negative effect occurs in the liver, which is represented by the element wood, it can cause a negative effect in the stomach, represented by the element earth.

There is today an epidemic of chronic disease of unknown cause. Not having a systematic approach to understanding the logic of the human body may be the primary factor contributing to this lack of knowledge. Having a system for understanding the relationships between the organs gives a greater chance of understanding the bigger picture of what the body is trying to do to achieve self-healing when it experiences abnormalities. From that systematic perspective, TCM's diagnostic system is philosophically ahead of modern medicine by 3000 years.

In ancient times, human inventions were few and simple. For the vast majority of the population, having systematic understanding of a field was rare. The Five Elements Theory was regarded as a form of metaphysics, and was something that very few people could understand. With electronic technology being so widespread now, most people have some concept of how systems work. The details of the Five Elements Theory no longer need to be memorised using the names of the elements, but can be understood logically and without mysticism. The theory is no different from early physics models before they were proven through rigorous testing, and it requires dedication from a large group of scientists to undertake the task of testing the TCM model. In an age where chronic diseases are rampant, that research direction might be worth a try as opposed to the reverse-engineering-based direction of modern medicine; and it might give us a better shot at uncovering the truth about the human body and developing true cures for chronic illnesses.

The meridian is the passageway for human body fluid

The body's meridians are thought to have several different functions, one of which is as passageways for body fluid ('lymph' in modern medicine). This concept was originally suggested by Chinese and Japanese researchers in the 'Body Fluid Passages of the Meridians Theory'. I have used those findings to create a household massage method which is explained in Chapter 6 and a related video. In the past several years, I have employed this method to help family and friends overcome their chronic illnesses. The method is easy to execute, as it does not require precision in targeting specific meridian points. You just have to work around the area of the meridian points for it to be effective. This makes it highly suitable for those without any expertise in massage to try at home.

As I have said, this massage method arose from the idea that 'the meridian is the passageway for human body fluid' and it works differently from most massage methods that aim to reduce stress in the muscles. The goal here is to increase the flow of the body's interior fluid, which in turn increases the functionality of the body. From a TCM perspective, fluidity of the meridians increases the functionality of the corresponding organs. Therefore, raising the effectiveness of corresponding organs is the purpose of this massage treatment. By improving the organ systems corresponding to the meridians, the body's state of health will naturally improve.

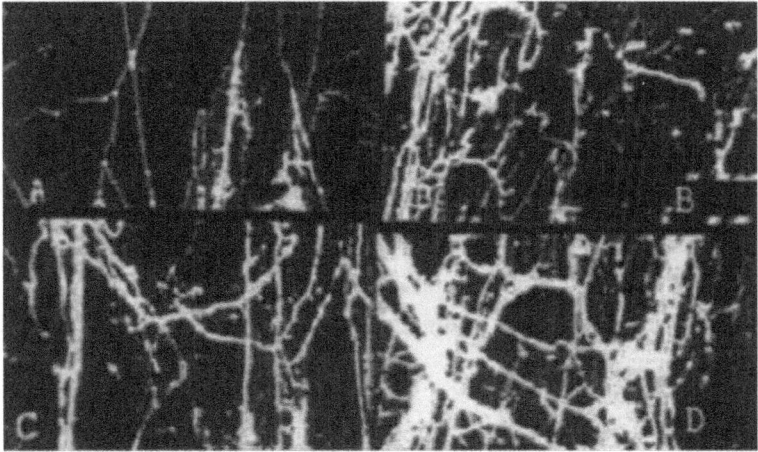

Figure 3.6: The random arrangement of capillaries at sites that are not near meridian points

According to Shanghai Fudan University's Professor Fei Lun and his team's research, while human capillaries appear to be randomly patterned throughout the body (Figure 3.6), those that are close to meridian points appear to run parallel to the meridians (Figure 3.7). Professor Lun's team discovered that this phenomenon, along with differences in blood pressure between meridian points along the same meridian, suggests that there is a flow passage between the meridian points where body fluid travels from meridian point to meridian point. In this scenario, the body fluid does not travel inside any blood vessel or capillary but rather within a flow passage located outside the blood vessels.

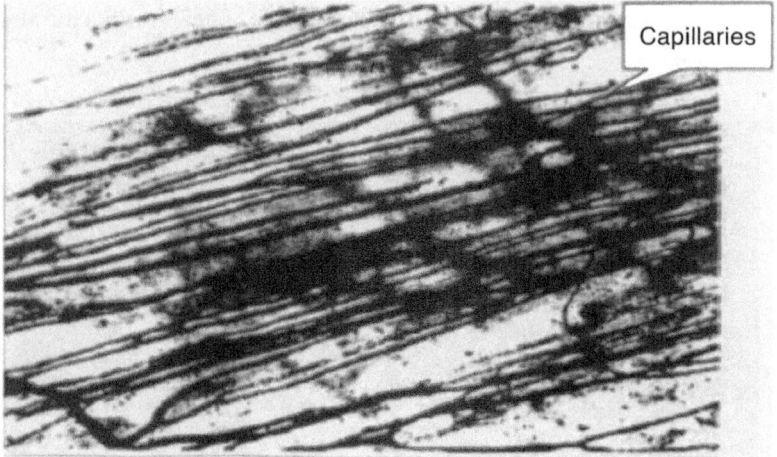

Capillaries

Figure 3.7: Capillaries running parallel to the meridians near meridian points

In Professor Fei Lun's experiment, micro-radioactive material was injected into certain parts of the body through which meridians are known to pass, to observe the movement of such material within the meridian. The experiment showed that the radioactive material did indeed move along the meridian path, which provides evidence in support of the theory that the meridian system is a series of body fluid flow passages that cover most of our body.

These passages serve a similar purpose to blood vessels and veins – to carry nutrients to and remove waste from body cells, as a backup system for blood vessels in the transferring of nutrients and wastes. The majority of our body cells are surrounded by body fluid. Nutrients travel from blood vessels to the smaller capillaries and are then eventually excreted from the capillary walls in body fluid (Figure 3.8). Body cells absorb nutrients within the body fluid and the process reverses for cell waste. The efficiency of the process of providing nutrients and removing wastes depends on the fluidity of these flow passages. Any reduction in the fluidity of meridians due to various pathogenic factors may lead to a variety of illnesses, including eczema, lupus, obesity, asthma and hair loss. These illnesses are caused by the body's inability to remove waste properly from the meridians, which is why improving meridian fluidity is one of the most important elements of any TCM healing process.

But how do we improve meridian fluidity? As we have seen, there are 12 main meridians and an assortment of minor meridians that run through our entire body. To improve the fluidity of all the meridians would be a very difficult task. Thus, we need to develop a method that is easy and effective.

In TCM, the bladder meridian is considered to be the main meridian that governs the removal of waste. It contains specific meridian points that correspond to all 12 meridians. We can imagine the bladder meridian as the main sewage system of the human body that gathers the cell waste from the other 11. The waste is transported to the kidneys and then to the bladder, where it is removed via urination. By improving the fluidity of the bladder meridian, we can improve the waste removal process as a whole, leading to the improvement of fluidity for all meridians.

This type of body fluid circulation is similar to ocean currents or wind drafts – we can observe ocean currents as along as the Earth is rotating. Flow through the meridians is active only while a person is alive – once movement and life stop, the current stops also. Dissection subjects have already lost their blood pressure, so all the body fluid has stopped moving. With our current technology, we are incapable of producing equipment that can monitor body fluid movement in a living person.

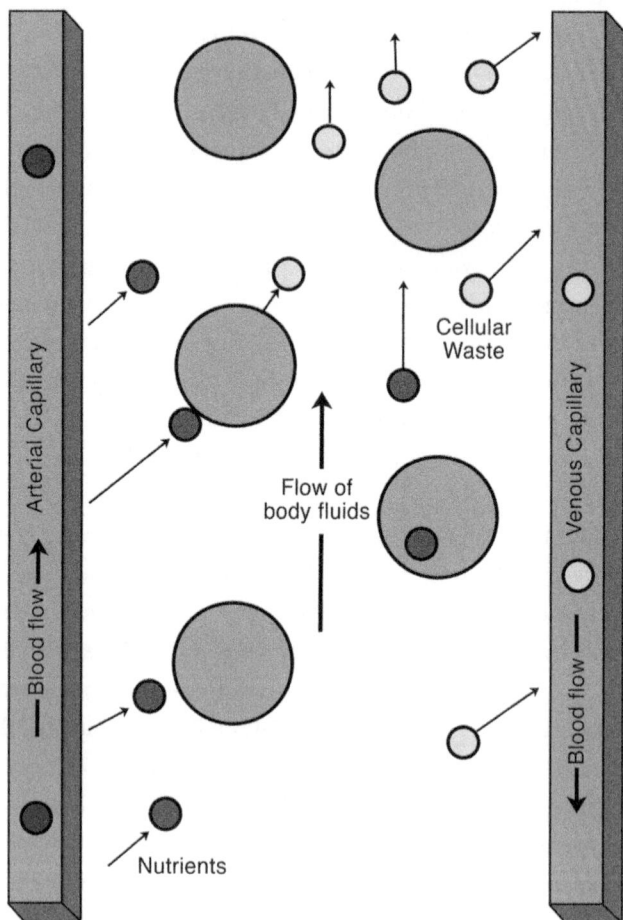

Figure 3.8: The movement of body fluid from the arterial to the venous bloodstreams

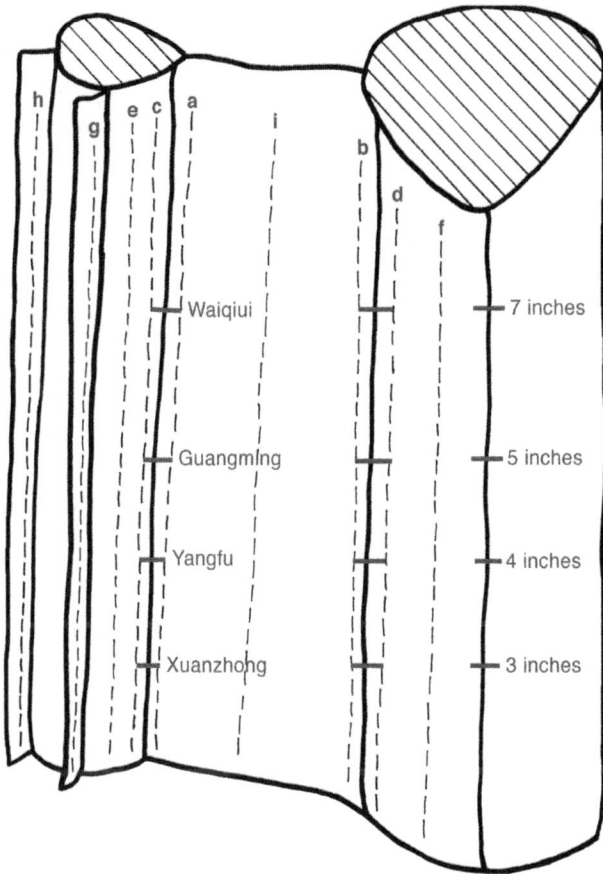

Figure 3.9: Corresponding meridian points on the gallbladder and stomach meridians – they occur at the same height on different meridians

Therefore, this body fluid model remains a theory, and while it can be mathematically calculated it cannot at the moment be seen.

The body's meridians run vertically – some from hands to head, some from head to feet, and some from feet to torso. The main passageways for body fluid within the meridians are between the bones and the periosteum (the membrane surrounding the bones). Therefore, most meridians are arranged along the bones. Another interesting phenomenon concerning meridian lines is that most points seem to be at the same height as their respective points on other meridian lines (Figure 3.9). If we link together the points of equal height, we end up with horizontal passages that circulate around the torso and the back, ending up at the bladder meridian.

This may mean that cellular waste material exits through one of two passageways. The first is through the veins and into the blood. It is circulated through the liver and spleen, which filter waste from the body. The other is through meridian flow, into the bladder meridian, and the bladder expels it from the body.

As I have explained, using the above logic, I have developed a series of massage techniques to improve the fluidity of the meridians; one is intended to improve the fluidity of the bladder meridian specifically (see page 103). These massage techniques are described in Chapter 6. By practising these techniques on a regular basis, significant improvements can be achieved in various chronic conditions.

The self-healing system

When following Traditional Chinese Medicine's methodology to treat chronic diseases, the main objective is to use any means available to improve the body's self-healing system, and to let it deal with the chronic condition itself. In other words, from a TCM perspective, the real doctor that deals with chronic diseases is the body's own self-healing system. The exterior doctor can act only as an assistant. Modern medicine, on the other hand, ignores the body's ability to handle problems. All chronic disease treatments are handled solely by doctors.

From my experience as an R&D engineer, when we are designing a more complicated product, maintenance is something that must be considered. A laptop, for instance, must have an opening at the back, and at the same time there must be easy consumer access for maintenance. Without these, it is very difficult for a product to have a decent life expectancy.

The human body is a product that can be used for decades, if not a full century. From a design perspective, it is far more complex and perfect than any man-made piece of machinery. To be able to last so long, it must have a near-perfect self-healing system that even as long ago as prehistoric times could last for several decades provided the person was not attacked and had enough nutritious food.

Even though the body has strong self-healing mechanisms built in to it, it may still exhibit illness from time to time. The main reason could be that the body's overall energy is too low, causing the self-healing system to malfunction. Alternatively, the symptoms could just be the effects of whatever processes the self-healing system needs to undergo.

Due to modern medicine's current inability to measure the body's total energy and TCM's lack of objective equipment to do so, the energy level of the patient can be determined only by observation. For example, with Asians in general, skin colour and texture are good indicators. TCM believes that a newborn baby has high levels of Blood and Qi. Older people have lower levels. So the closer a person's skin condition is to that of a baby, the higher the total energy level is thought to be. A baby's skin is soft and fresh. An older person's skin is dry and dim. Some may ask, 'But what if you have tanned skin?' The answer to this is in the texture. Tanned, healthy-looking skin has a smoother texture, whereas unhealthy skin is comparatively dry, rough and wrinkly.

Another telling indicator is the colour of the lips. A baby's lips are closer to pink, while an older person's are darker. There are other useful pointers, such as the state of the hair and eyes. These are all markers that TCM practitioners look for.

After a TCM practitioner has determined the patient's energy level, the patient will be asked about possible lifestyle changes that may have occurred prior to the emergence of symptoms. From that information, the trend in the patient's overall health is determined: upwards or downwards. From this it can be deduced whether the patient's body is suffering from an illness, or whether it is just undergoing maintenance. A decision about treatment can then be made.

The itching and swelling symptoms of a cut are part of a normal healing process. Because these symptoms happen on the outside, have short recovery cycles, and are fairly common, we readily understand that they are not part of an illness, but simply bodily maintenance at work. When the body is maintaining the organs, it is logical to think that there may also be uncomfortable symptoms. These uncomfortable symptoms, due to the fact that they are not on the surface and are therefore difficult to observe, may well be mistakenly classified as diseases. This misinterpretation stems from modern medicine's limited understanding of the self-healing system.

Raising the effectiveness of the body's self-healing system is one of the fundamental goals of TCM. Some treatments focus on reducing the symptoms caused by the self-healing system. TCM calls this 'tackling a problem on the surface'. Some treatments focus on raising the body's total energy level, which increases the efficiency and capabilities of the self-healing system, ultimately letting the body solve problematic illnesses by itself. TCM calls this 'dealing with the root of the problem'.

The logic of self-healing

Self-healing is an observable ability of the human body that we often overlook. We know that it plays a critical part in both internal and external injuries, since that is well known and documented. However, this is just the tip of the iceberg. Every part of our body is constantly in the process of breaking down. Using the analogy of the body as a computer, every time you use the computer, you are wearing it down little by little. Using it incorrectly only increases the amount of wear and tear. Similarly, the body also suffers daily wear and tear. The system that tries to minimise that problem and prolong the body's lifetime is the self-healing system.

When it comes to self-healing, TCM asserts that the body 'thinks' in terms of cost-benefit analysis. It asks itself questions such as: 'If I expend 100 units of energy on organ A, will that benefit be more than expending 100 units of energy on organ B?' If this were the only level of decision making, it would be obvious and unworthy of further discussion. But TCM goes a couple of steps further, asserting that the self-healing system can analyse the body's current situation, both internally and externally, and make complex and precise decisions about when and how to go about maintaining the organs.

A quick example to illustrate this process is how the body deals with psoriasis. From a TCM point of view, psoriasis is the equivalent of a car crash that has blocked an entire highway. The body recognises that there are damaged or unusable body tissues underneath the skin that need to be got rid of. It analyses possible exit routes and finds that the meridians are blocked; it would take far too much effort to transport all of the bodily debris through the blood so the solution it eventually arrives at is to remove the debris through the skin – this is the shortest distance and the most efficient approach. It then uses what energy it has to move the debris through the skin. When this process is complete, the body is rid of the debris, allowing better fluidity and functionality. (Of course, if the meridians for removing waste from under the skin remain blocked, there will be a continuous supply of debris to be cleared through the skin.)

Research papers on the body's self-healing system are few and scattered. Western research topics focus only on individual case studies of the self-healing system miraculously overcoming particular hard-to-cure diseases, without any systematic theories that try to explain the phenomenon. This is in large part due to the tremendous complexity of the human self-healing system and the fact that our current scientific approaches are not yet at a level where we can quantitatively organise its multi-tasking abilities into usable parameters to be measured and tested.

With that in mind, the only method available for establishing systematic logic is to use a combination of observational data and TCM theories to try to piece together a general logic of the human body. In the future, when more advanced tools of measurement for TCM approaches are made available (see Chapter 7 and the Appendix), we will be able to go back and test these theories quantitatively.

The concept of energy management

Just as we require energy to operate any independent system, the self-healing system needs energy as its most basic input. From observation we can see that the body manages its energy very precisely. It knows about the current energy distribution and uses that knowledge to make decisions about the recovery processes that it can currently execute.

Logic 1: The self-healing system separates its tasks into two categories: preventive maintenance and emergency maintenance

Ideally, your body only uses the energy generated each day. However, oftentimes through unhealthy living habits, your body ends up operating on a day-to-day deficit. When this happens, the body still must come up with the required quantity of energy to last through the day, so it taps into its reserves. While your body is using reserve energy, it keeps its regular maintenance to a minimum. It only chooses to carry out maintenance when it encounters problems that immediately threaten its life.

This is like the difference between maintaining your car and fixing it after it has broken down. Even if you do not carry out the recommended scheduled maintenance, your car can still run but with a higher likelihood of breaking down. Depending on your financial situation, you may or may not decide to maintain your car. Once your car has broken down, however, it will need to be fixed immediately for it to continue to operate.

The same goes for the body's self-healing system. Based on your current level of energy, it will make a set of decisions about what maintenance projects to take on, and with what priority. While your energy level is high, your organs will be maintained in the best condition. As your energy level drops, certain operations that have a lower priority will be abandoned out of necessity. Eventually, your self-healing system will perform only those tasks that are absolutely unavoidable, such as dealing with severe external bleeding or bacterial or viral infections.

This logic can explain why people in their prime who have unhealthy living habits due to a heavy workload, for example, will sometimes not get sick for long periods of time. It may be that the body is using its reserve energy, and its maintenance processes are suspended for the duration. Bodily maintenance often produces discomfort, and discomfort is often treated as illness. Only when the self-healing system takes a break will the user of the body not experience discomfort for long periods of time.

Logic 2: The effectiveness of self-healing is proportional to the body's energy level

Like most systems, the higher the energy, the higher the capabilities of that system. The body's energy level is reflected in how perfectly maintenance tasks are performed.

Traditional Chinese Medicine theories assert that when *cold Qi.* enters the body, it will first accumulate inside the outermost layer of skin. As the outer layers fill, the build-up gradually starts progressing inwards into the meridians, first the *Fu* meridians, and then the *Zang.* Eventually *cold Qi* enters the lungs. When we improve our lifestyle in such way that our body energy increases, the body will begin to remove the accumulated *cold Qi.* Since more energy is required to remove build-up that is deeper, as your energy level goes up, the build-up on your skin will be the first to be removed. You will then experience symptoms such as sneezing, runny nose, sore throat, and sometimes dizziness, fatigue, coughing and fever. Children naturally have a higher energy level, so they often experience more extreme symptoms, such as fevers. As we grow older, our energy level begins to decline, and we experience less extreme symptoms.

Cold Qi is an example of how the body manages its operations based on the amount of energy available. As the energy level goes down, so does the effectiveness of self-healing. Conversely, if we change long-term late-sleeping habits to sleeping early, and adjust our lifestyles in ways that improve our energy level, our self-healing system should become more and more effective.

The Yellow Emperor's Inner Canon describes in detail how to take care of the body properly through all four seasons. With changing seasons, the main variable is temperature. Winters are cold, so the body will distribute much of its energy in such a way that it keeps the cold from getting into its organs. At this time the body has no extra energy to invest in maintenance, so it will only handle problems that need to be addressed immediately. Regular maintenance work on the organs will be put on hold until spring.

If you do not dress warmly enough during winter, *cold Qi* will commonly get into your body, but your body may not show an immediate reaction. This is because the problem does not pose an immediate threat. Your body will store the build-up until springtime, when the temperature rises, allowing it to redistribute the energy used on heating. When that happens, your body will experience symptoms such as colds and fevers. People rarely connect *cold Qi* in the winter with the symptoms in springtime, so the effect is often overlooked. Since we do not connect the two, not wearing enough during winter becomes a habit, as we do not observe the direct consequences.

Different levels of body energy not only cause the self-healing system to work on different tasks, they also determine how completely each task will be accomplished. Many middle-aged people who improve their energy level begin to experience illnesses or discomforts that they have not experienced before. This is because at the time that the originating problem occurred, the body did not have sufficient energy to resolve the issue completely. When the energy level rises, the self-healing system resumes its work.

Logic 3: The self-healing system works on different organs depending on the level of energy or the season

From experience, maintenance of the heart is activated only at a very high energy level. Amongst the four seasons, summertime is when the body has access to most of its energy, so it is only then that the self-healing system can work on the heart.

It is rare to observe heart maintenance in adults. It is more common in children, mainly because their body is newer, so they naturally have a higher level of energy. If you suffer heatstroke during the summer, a condition that damages the heart, maintenance may take place during the same season or in the summer of the next year. That task usually occurs around 5 am to 7 am. Although it looks as if the person is in a very deep sleep, the body is actually distributing large amounts of its energy to fix the heart. The person will find it very difficult to wake up in the morning, and may sleep until noon if allowed. Sometimes, when children do not want to wake up in the summer, it may be because their body is fixing their heart, so parents should let them wake up naturally if possible.

Adults have lower energy levels, so unless they spend a long period of time nursing their energy level, it is very difficult for the body to fix potential heart problems.

Logic 4: Self-healing priorities

The priorities of the self-healing system must be such that, through repair of damaged organs, each organ's functionality is continually being improved. At the same time, the balance between the five *Zang* and five *Fu* meridians/organs must be maintained. To do this, the priorities system must have the ability to self-diagnose, always keeping tabs on which organs are in the worst shape.

As the weakest organ is repaired, its condition will gradually improve until eventually it is no longer the weakest organ. At that point, the self-healing system will finish the current maintenance cycle and move on to the new weakest organ. This creates a phenomenon whereby repair processes shift from organ to organ. The repair process creates various forms of discomfort depending on which organ is being repaired. The cyclical sequence of self-healing causes the body to experience shifts from symptom to symptom.

The body's self-healing priorities and our desired priorities are different. For example, people always want to eliminate problems that influence appearance as quickly as possible, such as obesity and skin diseases. However, the self-healing system considers survival and organ functionality first of all. From such a perspective, the odds of obesity or skin diseases killing you are far lower than those of problems involving the internal organs. So the body generally places these lesser problems on hold until all maintenance issues regarding the organs have been dealt with.

Logic 5: Meridian fluidity is a primary requirement for a fully functional self-healing system

In the earlier example of psoriasis, lack of meridian fluidity was cited as a source of the problem. By the same logic, increasing meridian fluidity becomes important in initiating self-healing of psoriasis. Through daily meridian massage, the fluids in the meridians can flow properly, successfully carrying the body's garbage outside. This removes the need for unwanted materials to exit through the skin, and psoriasis symptoms naturally disappear.

Observing the skin's recovery process, the body rejects dead material, which essentially becomes garbage. Since the garbage is generated on the exterior of the body, it simply falls off. When this same process occurs internally, garbage is also generated, but cannot simply fall off the skin. It needs to be dissolved in body fluid and sent through the circulatory system, eventually to exit via urination.

This newly created waste material puts stress on the body's waste removal system. The quality of blood in the veins will temporarily display abnormality as the level of waste in the blood increases. When the waste material successfully passes through the liver and kidneys and exits by urination, the quality of the blood will return to normal. At the same time, the waste in the meridians will increase. If the meridians are clogged to begin with, there may be pain in certain places. When that happens, it is best to massage the pericardium and bladder meridians (page 103), or add an appropriate amount of exercise to increase the meridians' ability to remove waste.

To sum up the logic of the self-healing system, improving Blood and Qi is the key to triggering and sustaining the self-healing system. Increasing fluidity of the meridians then helps transport the garbage created by self-healing activity out of the body. This means the body can function cleanly and efficiently, while not allowing the piling up of garbage to impede organ functionality, which could result in chronic illnesses.

The main difference between boosting the self-healing system and having doctors deal with illnesses directly is that improving the self-healing system does not treat any particular illness; instead it raises the body's functionality as a whole. Improving Blood and Qi and taking out bodily waste are the most important methods of strengthening the self-healing system, and keys to healthy living.

氣 血

CHAPTER
4

Enabling the self-healing system to cure psoriasis and stop hair loss

Psoriasis is a common chronic skin condition that affects approximately 2-4% of the world's population. The symptoms are usually red and white scaly patches on the top layer of the skin. These patches will gradually peel off over time, accompanied by constant itching, swelling and pain. Imagine a never-healing wound where scabs form and fall off over and over again. The causes of the disease, like those of most other chronic diseases, are unknown. Western medicine defines it as an immune-mediated disease. As with most other chronic diseases, there is no cure and it can be controlled only by using constant medication, although in the most severe cases there are no effective methods of controlling the symptoms. People with severe psoriasis often suffer both physically and emotionally, as the disease damages the patient's appearance. Many of these patients tend to wear long-sleeved clothing and head gear to cover the affected areas in order to keep the symptoms hidden while in public.

One of my relatives in Taiwan developed psoriasis about three years ago. Through her healing process, my understanding of the disease was broadened and the theory of TCM was reaffirmed. My relative's psoriasis was on her scalp, underarms, forearms, chest, back and lower legs. Though the affected areas were not particularly large, they were, as I have described, spread out across various parts of her body. During the early stages, when the symptoms first appeared, she went to several hospitals and received different opinions from doctors. When the diagnosis of psoriasis was eventually confirmed, she was devastated by the news. 'I still have the little pamphlet explaining the disease that I got from the hospital right after the diagnosis,' she said. 'On the first page of the pamphlet it said "**Psoriasis cannot be cured**, but through medication the symptoms can be reduced." The thought that I'd have to live with this condition for the rest of my life was awful. Not only was the disease not curable, but the likelihood of the symptoms becoming worse over time was extremely distressing.'

When analysing the disease on her behalf, I used three major TCM concepts: (1) the lungs govern the skin; (2) the skin is a main detox passage for the body; and (3) the meridians are passageways for body fluids.

Concept 1

The first concept was the TCM theory that the lungs govern the skin. TCM asserts that the lung system, meaning both the organ and the meridian, governs the distribution of water in the body. This is not to say that the lung system is responsible for the physical distribution of water, but rather that it governs the body's function in distributing water. When the body's lung system is low in energy, the body will lack the ability to distribute water properly. The most recognisable symptom is dry skin. Our skin requires a certain amount of moisture to protect its surface. When skin dryness occurs, the skin becomes vulnerable to various skin diseases. Moreover, a lack of water within the body will cause the meridians to become less fluid, making it difficult for the body to remove waste within the meridian. A build-up of waste inside the lung meridian will also create various skin conditions.

Concept 2

The second TCM concept that I used says that the skin is the main detox passage for the body alongside the liver and the kidneys. In other words, a sizeable proportion of the body's toxins are released through the skin. A major source of toxins in the body is the intake of inorganic substances. As we observe in nature, only plants are able to absorb inorganic nutrients such as minerals directly from the ground. Animals can absorb these nutrients only indirectly, either by consuming plants or by consuming other animals that have absorbed these plants. The same goes for humans. With the exception of salt and water, most of the food sources we consume are organic. I do not think any of us have ever been at a dinner table where we were served rocks or metal to eat. Thus, it is reasonable to believe that the laws of nature dictate we should consume organic foods rather than inorganic. However, due to modern-day science, the amount of inorganic substances that humans consume has increased (see below). The human body can digest and process some of the inorganic substances it consumes, but others will become toxins in the body. Luckily, our body has a superb detox system. Through our liver and kidneys, it is able to remove toxins. But the detox process may sometimes become the cause of some common skin conditions.

This is because one of the main passages for disposing of toxins is through the skin. When our skin comes into contact with inorganic substances, it absorbs them as toxins but it is able to remove them through the skin instead of utilising the internal detox system of the liver and kidneys. One analogy that I use is the common toxicity found in fish skin. Fish skin often becomes toxic when the water the fish lives in is polluted. The human body is also able to prevent toxic material from entering its internal organs. It makes sense that it works this way since these toxins can cause major damage to our kidneys and liver. The removal of toxic substances is the cause of various chronic skin conditions. In other words, some skin diseases are merely the symptom or the side-effect of our body's detox process.

In the modern world, our lives are filled with inorganic and toxic materials. Processed foods, in particular, are one of the main sources of toxins for modern-day humans. In order to lower costs and maintain a uniform product, food companies will often include chemical-based food additives in their products. The research that is done to ensure these additives have no long-term ill effects on human health is often limited. It is also extremely difficult to prove there is a correlation between these additives and various diseases. Since animals do not consume inorganic substances in nature, perhaps it is not to our benefit to consume these substances either.

Besides food, there are many other sources of toxins in our daily lives. Common cosmetic products such as hair gel and hair dye contain harmful chemicals that may enter through contact with our skin. Home detergent as well as home cleaning products may also contain harmful chemicals. Living in the modern world, absorbing toxins is inevitable. However, that does not mean we should give up any attempt at a healthy lifestyle. We should use this knowledge to limit the toxins that our body ingests and improve our body's detox functions, so it can remove these toxins once they have entered it.

Concept 3

The third concept that I used in healing my relative's psoriasis is the concept of our meridians as passageways for body fluid. The fluidity of our meridians determines our body's ability to pass nutrients to and remove waste from our cells. If our meridians become congested, the body will no longer be able to remove waste properly through these passages. The additional waste that clogs our meridians over time may become the source of the symptoms of psoriasis.

Redefining the symptoms of psoriasis

Another important step in analysing psoriasis besides using the above TCM concepts is to rethink the disease as a whole. It is crucial to review the symptoms of psoriasis in relation to the cause of the disease. The central logic of modern medicine in its response to diseases is to assume that the symptoms are a sign of body malfunction, possibly caused by external pathogens. Sometimes, when such pathogens are absent, the malfunction is taken to be caused autonomously. TCM takes a different approach to the problem and assumes that the body is intelligent and that it has a strong self-healing system. When reviewing a symptom of any disease, TCM considers the possibility that the symptom may be caused by the self-healing process rather than simply being the result of bodily malfunction. When we consider that the symptoms of psoriasis may be the result of the body's self-healing process, the possibility of a complete cure for the disease emerges.

The path to curing psoriasis

Let us therefore assume that the symptoms of psoriasis are the result of the body's self-healing process. During the process of removing toxins via the skin, the body develops the various symptoms of psoriasis. Methods of healing the disease become apparent; the body needs to do the following two things:

1. Reduce or eliminate the intake of the toxins that are causing the condition.

2. Allow the body to complete the removal of the toxins that are already in the body.

Examining my cousin's daily habits, I discovered that she had dyed her hair for the past 15 years. Hair colouring, as we know, involves treatment of the hair with various chemical compounds. Since a large proportion of her psoriasis symptoms were located on her scalp, it was reasonable to suspect that the toxins might be related to the hair-dye chemicals. Moreover, she had a habit of using hair spray for hairstyling. Hairspray is another product that is mostly made up of inorganic chemicals.

With these possible causes in mind, I formulated a plan for healing her psoriasis:

1. Make sure that she received adequate sleep so that her body could maintain a high level of body energy. This is essential for the body to proceed with its self-healing process.

2. Reduce the intake of toxins. In this particular case, she was to stop using hair colouring and hairspray. Besides abandoning hair products, she made a serious effort to improve her daily diet by reducing the intake of food additives and preservatives.

3. Daily massage of the bladder meridian and daily hair combing. The bladder meridian is essential in the process of removing waste. Making sure the meridian is fluid will help the body speed up the detox process. Hair combing follows the same idea. Since most of the symptoms were located on her scalp, hair combing could improve the meridian fluidity near the affected area.

It is important to note that the healing process may be lengthy. There may be no apparent progress in the first few weeks or months. In my relation's case, after the first month of following the above three points of healing, she did not experience any changes to the affected areas. However, she noted that while the areas already affected by psoriasis did not improve, there was no spread to additional areas. After six months of massage and healthy living, the affected areas gradually began to reduce. In the next three months, the psoriasis on her arms and legs disappeared. The psoriasis that was on her scalp took a further three months to go. Within about one year from the start of applying these methods, her psoriasis was completely cured.

For my relative, the first six months of the treatment were the most difficult. Because progress was minimal, she often questioned the effectiveness of my approach and the validity of the reasoning and considered returning to modern medications. I encouraged her to employ a nothing-to-lose attitude in confronting these doubts. First of all, there is no scientific proof that psoriasis will worsen without treatment. Secondly, the current medical treatments are aimed at containing the symptoms rather than curing the disease and in some cases, these treatments will merely lead to increased symptoms in the long run. Why not attempt to cure the disease first, before using the conventional methods? After all, if my methods had not worked, she could still have gone back to the default treatment.

Doubt is the greatest deterrent to the success of this treatment. On several occasions, my relative felt disappointed at the lack of progress and even when it did occur, she questioned whether it was sustainable or if the improvement was just temporary. Only when the psoriasis on her scalp had mostly gone and the bald spots that were caused by the condition were filled with new hair did my relative feel confidence in these methods.

After the successful experience with my relative, I was able to advise many others who were troubled by psoriasis and many of them achieved various degrees of success in healing their condition. I also shared the story on my website and received many positive emails regarding its effectiveness. While I do not claim that this method is suitable for all sufferers, as there are many forms of psoriasis as well as people who are genetically predisposed to it, this is nevertheless a method built on the foundation of TCM philosophy. From my personal experience, it is generally effective in curing the condition. If you are not content with containing the disease by the use of drugs to avert its symptoms, I encourage you to try this method, which offers the possibility of a complete cure.

Hair loss: my own experience

Hair loss is a common condition in men over the age of 30. In recent years, studies have shown that hair loss is starting at a younger age, which suggests that it is a major issue in today's world. While in itself not life threatening, it may indicate other health issues. I would like to share my own experiences with hair loss and the insight that I have gained in explaining its causes.

I experienced hair loss when I was around 35 years old. As I recall, at the time, every morning when I woke up I would discover strands of hair on my pillow. As any other man in his 30s would be, I was distraught at this sudden loss of hair and tried many different methods to stop it. At first I suspected it was food-related. MSG was commonly used in cooking in Taiwan at the time and I suspected that it might be the cause. However, after I eliminated MSG from my diet, my condition continued to worsen. I tried various other food therapies as well as some common hair restoration products, yet none was successful in stopping the hair loss. What began as a receding hairline led to balding of the entire front area of my head by the age of 40. By the time I was 45, the only hair I had left was on the back of my head and along the temporal area. The front and center areas of my head were completely bald.

As I learned more about TCM and developed a deeper understanding of the human body, I began to understand the reason behind my hair loss. Through many years of changing my living habits and practising various healing methods, I was able to stop my hair loss and even to grow hair back in some areas that were bald. Throughout this process I realised that while it is much more difficult to restore hair in areas that are completely bald, slowing down the rate of hair loss or even stopping it is much easier. I believe that this knowledge is especially helpful for those who are in the early stages of hair loss, as the problem can easily be solved following TCM-based methods.

The cause of my hair loss can be attributed to two things – the thinness of my hair strands and the thickness of my scalp. Studies have shown that the average person's hair is around 0.05~0.15 mm in diameter. I remember measuring my own hair using a mechanical draft ruler, back when I was still a college student, and my hair measured 0.05~0.06 mm, which was at the lower end of the average hair diameter range. TCM attributes the thinness of hair to a weakness of the kidney system and asserts that the cause is mostly hereditary. There is an old saying in Chinese: 'Kidney *Qi* is the *Qi* before birth'. As I have explained, the concept of *Qi* is synonymous with energy which, when used to describe a particular organ system, means the general condition of the system. So the condition of the kidney system is determined before birth. Hereditary reasons aside, poor living habits – such as lack of sleep and over-exhaustion – can cause the kidney system to weaken as well. My own weakness in the kidneys was a combination of hereditary factors and being late to bed. I remember that after I started going to college, I rarely went to bed before midnight. Constantly going to bed late lowered my body energy, which contributed to the weakening of my kidney system and therefore to the thinness of my hair.

The second reason for my baldness was the thickness of my scalp. Several meridians travel through the scalp. The bladder meridian, as well as the gallbladder meridian, has passages that travel through this area (see Figure 6.1). These meridians tend to become less fluid as a result of an abundance of *cold Qi* (see page 31) absorbed by the scalp. Over time, these clogged meridians lead to the scalp becoming thicker, which hinders hair growth.

The absorption of *cold Qi* occurs when the head is exposed to cold. Certain habits tend to contribute to this problem. The habit of not blowing your hair dry after a shower is one of the most common causes. A lot of men, myself in the past included, wash our hair and then tend to let it dry naturally. People who do that on a regular basis will likely develop a thick layer of fat underneath the scalp. We can test this by pressing two fingers down on the top of the head. The thickening feels like a layer of jelly between the scalp and the skull, whereas with a thin and healthy scalp, one can easily feel the skull without much resistance. The thick layer under the scalp is a sign that the meridians in that region have lost their fluidity. A clogged meridian makes it more difficult for the hair follicles to absorb nutrients. Over time, these hair follicles will lose their function due to a lack of nutrients and gradually become dormant, resulting in hair loss.

After practising hair-combing for over a year, along with healthy living habits, I noticed a significant thinning of my scalp tissue. As my scalp returned to its original healthy condition, areas of my head that were previously bald began to grow thin strands of hair. While I do not expect my hair to return to the lushness that it had when I was in my 20s, the hair that I have now is significantly more than when I was 50.

As I have discovered from my own experiences and the experiences of people who have tried my method of hair combing, back massages and healthy living, it is much easier to stop hair loss than it is to regrow hair when one is already bald. If someone has just discovered that he or she is experiencing hair loss, by practising hair combing and taking simple precautions, such as always blow-drying hair, they can stop the process of hair loss in a matter of weeks.

氣 血

CHAPTER
5

Applying the principles of Traditional Chinese Medicine to treating obesity

According to a recent report from the United Nations Food and Agricultural Organization, the United States has the highest obesity rate of all developed nations. Standing at 38.2%, the US is followed mostly closely by Mexico at 32.4%.

While some blame the problem of obesity in the United States on the prevalence of its fast-food culture and inactive lifestyles, from TCM's point of view it is not difficult to see why Americans may be more prone to obesity than people in other countries. It is interesting to note that of the top 30 most obese countries, none is in the East Asian cultural sphere that includes China, Korea, Taiwan, Japan, Vietnam, Mongolia, Malaysia and Singapore. This is not because people in those countries have particularly active lifestyles or do not share the Americans' love

Country	Prevalence
United States	38.2
Mexico	32.4
New Zealand	30.7
Australia	27.9
United Kingdom	26.9
South Africa	26.5
Germany	23.6
Ireland	23.0
Russian Federation	19.6
France	15.3
China	7.0
India	5.0

Table 5.1: Percentage of population over 15 years who were obese in 2015 (Obesity Update, OECD 2017)

of fast-food, but rather that there are certain health and other cultural practices that make them less prone to obesity.

Before we try to understand how it is some cultures rather than others can lead to obesity, let us first discuss the causes of obesity from TCM's point of view.

The relationship between obesity and heart disease is well known and accepted by the general public. However, in terms of cause and effect, TCM's and Western medicine's views on this subject are completely different. Western medicine believes that people who are obese have an increased risk of heart disease. In other words, being overweight is a likely cause of heart disease. TCM's point of view on this relationship is the reverse: people who have heart disease are more likely to develop obesity. In other words, heart disease is the cause of obesity.

The reason for the difference of opinion lies in the diagnosis of heart disease or, more specifically, the time period for the diagnosis. Pulse diagnosis is one of the most common diagnostic techniques used in TCM. Using pulse diagnosis, skilled TCM doctors are able to detect heart abnormalities much earlier than by using methods employed by modern medicine. This isn't to say that pulse diagnosis is more accurate or more reliable than modern instruments such as an electrocardiogram (ECG) or echocardiogram (Echo), but it is a much more common practice during TCM's diagnostic procedure, so the signs of heart problems are likely to be detected much earlier. Pulse diagnosis is, for example, extremely effective in detecting a condition called pericardial effusion (fluid around the heart). It can often detect this in patients even before they experience symptoms associated with it, such as shortness of breath and palpitations. The main diagnostic method in modern medicine is by physical examination, in which the doctor listens for abnormal sounds from the heart. Unless the patient has significant symptoms of pericardial effusion, the problem is rarely detected unless he or she undergoes ECG or Echo procedures. This difference in diagnostic sensitivity extends to various other heart diseases. To confirm, as a good TCM doctor is able to detect heart abnormalities before the symptoms become detectable by the patient, TCM is likely to diagnose a patient with heart problems much earlier than Western medicine does in practice.

With that in mind, let us go back to the relationship between obesity and heart disease. Because of early heart disease detection, TCM is able to observe patients with the early stages of heart disease. Obesity is often an outcome for these patients, therefore TCM is able to conclude that there is a relationship between obesity and heart disease. Since obesity generally happens much later than heart disease, it seems to be the result rather than the cause. Conversely, because modern medicine detects heart disease during its later stages, when the symptoms are already apparent and obesity already present, obesity is seen as the cause rather than the result.

To understand the relationship better, we first need to understand the difference between what TCM and modern medicine view as the cause of obesity. Modern medicine views obesity as simply a lack of energy balance, meaning energy in is not equal to energy out. Energy in is the amount of energy or calories you get from food and drinks, and energy out is the amount of energy that your body spends on body functions and activities such as breathing, digesting, sports etc. If a person's energy in is more than their energy out, then they will gain weight when the left over energy is stored as fat. While TCM agrees that people will gain weight if they consume more calories than they use, it asserts that the biggest factor in obesity is how efficiently a person's body is able to use energy and excrete waste. TCM suggests that several factors can influence how efficiently the person's body is able to burn off excess energy and excrete waste. As obesity occurs when the body loses its ability to perform such tasks, TCM's treatment focuses mainly on improving and restoring the body's ability to burn off calories and remove waste.

In the next sections I will go into detail on how TCM treats obesity. The treatment can be divided into two parts: improving the efficiency of the heart and spleen and improving the fluidity of the meridians.

Poorly functioning heart and spleen systems are the main cause of obesity

TCM views the heart as the most important organ in the human body. Of the five major internal organs, or the five *Zangs* (heart, liver, spleen, lungs, kidneys), the heart is the foremost. Its importance lies in its ability to pump the blood that directly impacts upon the functionality of the four other major organs.

According to TCM theory, the spleen system plays an important part in two major body functions: the transport of body fluid and the functioning of the immune system. The transport of body fluid is crucial during our body's waste removal process. A spleen system that is overworked or malfunctioning will cause a delay in the body's waste removal process. Over time, that delay will cause excess waste to remain throughout the body, leading to excess fat. An overworked spleen system occurs when a person's immune system is consistently being overstressed. The immune system can become overstressed when the person has lengthy bouts of internal infections. A typical infection comes from unclean food or drink. Raw foods, especially raw fish or beef, often contain parasites. Frequent ingestion of such foods will lead to frequent parasitic infections in the digestive system, which may result in an overstressed immune system. In women, chronic gynecological infections and poor postpartum care may also lead to a poor spleen system due to constant bouts of infections.

The functionality of the spleen system will affect the functionality of the heart system via the pericardium. The pericardium is a double-walled sac that surrounds and covers the heart. Between the pericardium and the heart is pericardial fluid, which acts as cushioning as well as lubrication for the heart so that it can move freely within the pericardium. When the spleen system is overworked due to infection or low body energy, the spleen system's ability to transport water declines, which then leads to an increase in the pericardial fluid. An excess of pericardial fluid will limit the flexibility of the pericardium, which will reduce the heart's ability to pump blood. As the heart's ability declines, there is a negative effect on the functionality of the four other main organs; this becomes a vicious cycle as the decline of the heart will further decrease the spleen's ability to transport water, which will then cause an increase in the pericardial fluid, and the cycle will lead back to the decline in heart function.

As the condition continues to worsen, the person will become more and more obese as the body is unable to remove waste water efficiently. As heart function continues to decline, the person will eventually experience noticeable heart-related symptoms, such as irregular heartbeat or palpitations, as well as high blood pressure. If the person then visits a doctor and undergoes heart examination, it is likely that a variety of heart diseases will be diagnosed. While it appears that the heart disease may be due to obesity, when we follow TCM theory it is easy to see that the person's heart problems actually began prior to becoming obese.

Activities or habits that may contribute to spleen weakness

Now that I've explained how the decline of spleen and heart functioning contributes to obesity, let us examine the various daily activities and living habits that may cause this decline.

Unclean diet

Some of the most common infections occur in our digestive system, caused by the foods we eat as well as the methods that we use to eat them. Given that people generally develop dietary habits that do not readily change, these infections may become a chronic problem, as someone who practises poor dietary habits will experience repeat infections.

The most common form of infection comes from eating raw foods, particularly raw meats or fish. Parasites are a common and natural occurrence in fish. When eating raw or undercooked fish, the risk is high that a person will contract parasitic diseases. While certain preventive measures are taken in the preparation of raw fish dishes such as sushi and sashimi, these dishes still carry a much higher risk of containing parasites when compared with cooked fish. In order to completely eliminate parasites, the fish must be frozen at a temperature of -20°C for at least seven days. Since most kitchens do not have the proper equipment to reach such temperatures, eating raw fish will likely come with the risk of infection. Similar infections also occur in the consumption of undercooked pork, poultry, beef and other meats.

It is important to remember that while the symptoms of these infections may not always be noticeable, if a person ingests pathogens by consuming raw foods, the body's immune system will always be working to defeat them. To put it simply, one may not always notice the consequences of ingesting unclean foods, but the damage done to the body by such food will still occur. When a person's body defends itself against these pathogens, the spleen system will become overworked, leading to the vicious cycle described earlier (see page 52).

Besides eating raw foods, infection via saliva is another common problem. Adult mouths may contain between 500 and 1000 different types of bacteria. The particular combination found in any one person will be unique. In other words, it is unlikely that two human beings will have exactly the same oral ecology. In instances where saliva is exchanged, cross-contamination between different oral ecologies can cause infection. This form of cross-infection commonly occurs during group dining where eating utensils are shared, or in Chinese dining where chopsticks are used. In traditional Chinese dining, food dishes are shared amongst all the people at the table and each person uses their chopsticks to transfer food from the main dish to their plate or bowl. Each person then uses the same chopsticks to consume food on their plate.

Infection via saliva is particularly harmful to children, especially young infants, who have far fewer bacteria in their mouths than adults;

a sudden cross-contamination of saliva between adult and child can be much more damaging for the child. Thus it is recommended that children have separate eating utensils and parents are encouraged to avoid any unnecessary exchange of saliva with their children.

Gynecological infections

In women, a common cause of stress to the spleen system may come from reccurring gynecological infections, specifically infections of the vagina, cervix and uterus. Because these can occur repeatedly, women who suffer from these ailments will also suffer from the overstressing of their spleen system. It is difficult to prevent such infections. Besides the obvious method of practising good feminine hygiene, having a healthy lifestyle (sleeping early, proper diet) will help to increase body energy and improve the immune system so that the body can better defend itself and recover from those infections.

Postpartum recovery care

The methods of care used in the postpartum (after giving birth) period differ greatly between Western and Chinese cultures. In the former, not enough emphasis is placed on postpartum care compared with Chinese societies. When we use TCM theories to examine the effect of a lack of postpartum care, it is easy to see some of the long-term damage this can do to a woman and how the damage can lead to obesity.

Giving birth takes a heavy toll on a woman's body. Whether the method is a natural vaginal delivery or a Caesarean section, a significant amount of haemorrhaging and scarring is expected during and after childbirth. Thus it is important for a woman to take care of her body at this time so that it has sufficient time and a supportive environment in which to recuperate. During this period, it is natural for the spleen system to be under constant stress because the body must heal the wound(s) that it sustained during delivery. Therefore it is recommended that the woman should increase rest as well as adjust her diet and lifestyle in order to minimise stress. Failing to do so may cause long-term damage to the spleen system as well as to the kidney system. Both these systems are important in the body's waste removal process. As described earlier, the spleen system governs the transportation of the body fluid that carries the body's waste material. The kidneys govern the final stage of the waste removal process – that is, the excretion of the waste product through urination. Thus damage done to either one of these two systems will cause a disturbance in the body's waste removal process, which can lead to obesity. Such damage may not be apparent at the outset, but the symptoms will begin to show as the woman approaches menopause. In other words, TCM believes that women who did not receive proper postpartum care are more likely to gain weight after menopause, because of the damage that was done to their spleen and kidney systems during the postpartum period, which has reduced their body's waste removal function.

In Chinese cultures, women typically rest for 30 days after giving birth. During that period there are specific rules governing diet and living conditions that the postpartum woman must follow to ensure proper recovery. The details of Chinese postpartum care are too specific for this book and widely available online. I suggest all my readers take the time to research these methods as they are generally effective.

Drinking iced water as a cause of obesity

The relationship between iced water and obesity is a difficult one to understand and accept, especially without any prior knowledge of Traditional Chinese Medicine. In my experience of conveying this concept to people, the first reaction has generally been that such a thing is impossible. Water, as we know, contains no calories, thus it is impossible to become obese from drinking water. While I agree that the water itself does not cause obesity, the process of drinking iced water may do so.

As discussed earlier, the proper functioning of the heart and spleen systems is essential in the body's waste removal process. A disturbance in either system will have a negative impact, resulting in obesity. Drinking iced water or, more specifically, drinking iced water under particular circumstances, may cause significant damage to the heart system.

Having an ice-cold glass of water when the outdoor temperature is high, or directly after exhausting exercise, is a common practice for many people. Most people enjoy the experience because drinking cold water in high temperature helps the body to cool down at an accelerated pace. What people do not realise is that this activity carries the hidden danger of damaging the heart. To understand how that occurs, we need first to understand how our body deals with heat.

The human body can function only within a specific range of body temperatures. When the body temperature rises above the acceptable range, it can cause body proteins and cell membranes to be damaged or destroyed, which will then lead to severe symptoms and death. The body prevents itself from overheating by using two methods to cool down, both of which rely heavily on the heart.

The first method of cooling is radiation. Heat behaves like water flowing downhill. As long as the air temperature surrounding the body is lower than the body temperature, heat will radiate from the body to the air. However, the transfer of heat slows down or stops as the gap between air temperature and body temperature narrows. This radiation mechanism requires the circulatory system to reroute blood flow so that more blood travels to the skin. The second method of cooling is through sweat evaporation. Every droplet of sweat that evaporates from the skin will carry away heat from the body. However, besides removing heat, sweat also carries sodium, potassium and other essential minerals away from the body, which may cause a chemical imbalance. To counter these losses, the heart must pump faster and harder as the body secretes hormones to help the body hold on to water and minerals.

The heart is central to the body's cooling process, relying heavily on the effectiveness of that process to maintain temperature and avoid overheating. A person drinking iced water immediately after exhausting exercise causes a major disturbance to the body's cooling process. As the iced water enters the mouth, the cold sensation that is felt in the mouth confuses the brain into believing that the body has cooled down and no longer requires as much cooling as it actually does. The result is that the body will prematurely terminate the cooling process, believing that it has already cooled off. This disturbance causes damage to the heart because the heart itself is unable to receive sufficient cooling.

Chew your food

In today's world, obesity is a major issue for many countries, as shown in Table 5.1. The main focus is on the diet of the individual and his or her exercise regimen, and very little has been said about how *styles* of eating relate to obesity. The term 'healthy eating' rarely refers to the method and speed of food consumption. In my opinion, while choosing the right food is important in building a healthy diet, eating slowly and chewing your food properly are no less important.

The human body requires key nutrients that are derived from

the foods we eat. However, simply eating is not enough. The rate of nutrient absorption determines the efficiency of our eating process. In a hypothetical scenario where two people with a similar body type have the same diet, the person with a higher nutrient absorption rate will be able to acquire key nutrients from a smaller amount of food. In the long run, the amount of food we eat and the type of food our body craves will be relative to our body's ability to acquire the essential nutrients. So increasing our body's nutrient absorption rate should be one of the main steps toward developing a healthy diet.

How properly chewing your food increases nutrient absorption

Our body's absorption of nutrients mostly occurs when the food reaches the small intestine. Foods that are not properly digested will not be able to pass through the wall of the small intestine and will instead exit the body as waste.

The action of chewing food plays an important part in determining whether food is properly digested. Firstly, if a food particle is too large when it reaches the small intestine, it will not be able to pass through the intestinal wall. By chewing food properly we ensure that it can be fully broken down in the stomach. Secondly, chewing food ensures sufficient secretion of bile, which is essential in the digestion of fats.

Bile is produced continuously by the liver and stored and concentrated in the gallbladder; from there it is discharged into the duodenum after food has been ingested. The effectiveness of the gallbladder is related to the fluidity of the gallbladder meridian. A person whose gallbladder meridian is congested will have trouble with bile secretion. When we examine the gallbladder meridian, we will notice that a major portion travels across the cheek area. During the process of chewing food, our facial muscles will naturally massage the gallbladder meridian in that area, which will make it more fluid. So by chewing our food properly, we can ensure that our bile secretion is sufficient.

I recommend chewing each bite of food at least 20 times before swallowing. If we can develop this habit, we will be certain of properly digesting food both physically (breaking food down into smaller pieces) and chemically (prompting sufficient bile secretion to dissolve fats). Proper digestion increases our nutrient absorption rate, as a higher percentage of food can be absorbed through the wall of the small intestine. When the body can absorb sufficient nutrients even when the amount of food it ingests decreases, controlling calorie intake becomes easier as our appetite naturally becomes smaller. The practice of chewing food properly should be the foundation of any weight-loss programme.

Now it is time to introduce you to the massage programme for promoting meridian fluidity that I have mentioned earlier.

氣 血

CHAPTER
6

Daily massages

In order to improve the fluidity of the meridians and thereby body energy, I have developed a series of massages that can be carried out daily. They are simple to do and are safe for people without training in massage techniques to practise. For a thorough explanation of how to perform each massage, please refer to the video at https://www.youtube.com/watch?v=79mu7LOplqQ&feature=youtu.be for more detailed directions.

Daily massage 1: Hair combing

The practice of hair combing as part of a healthy-living regimen has been around in China, and many other countries, for hundreds of years. Chinese women in ancient times used a type of comb called a *Bie* to comb their hair. They used hair combing with essential oils as a substitute for washing hair, since catching a cold from having wet hair was relatively dangerous, especially to those who were not wealthy. A lack of heating and food made the recovery process a potentially difficult one, with a high risk of complications. Women therefore took what measures they could to avoid catching a cold in the first place. During the winter in particular, the process of washing and drying hair was risky so combing with sweet olive oil was developed as an alternatives. Traditional Chinese Medicine practitioners of those times discovered that besides the obvious benefits of improving hair quality, hair combing could improve the fluidity of the meridians in the head area. Hence it became more than just a way to improve personal hygiene. It was a health practice in itself.

Several important meridians pass through the head (see Figure 6.1). At the centre of the head lies the *Du* meridian, and close beside it on each side the two bladder meridians. On both sides of the head lie the gallbladder meridians. Normally it is difficult to massage these meridians since these areas are covered by hair, but using combs or firm brushes we can gently massage these areas in the correct direction for meridian flow (front to back).

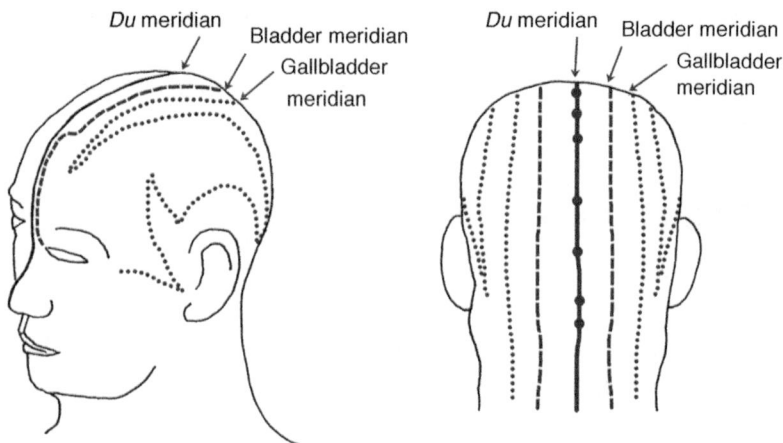

Figure 6.1: Back and side views of the head showing the position of the central *Du* meridian and the two bladder and gallbladder meridians

Before combing, we need to make sure that we have chosen a suitable comb or brush. It is important to find one that can deliver a firm yet gentle pressure. The tip of the comb must not be pointy or sharp as it may damage the scalp. Furthermore, in 'combing' the forehead where there is no hair a *gua sha* board (see Figure 6.2) should be used instead.

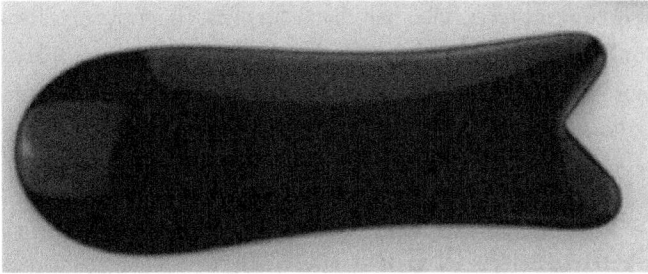

Figure 6.2: *Gua sha* board

Comb along these five meridians (*Du*, two bladder and two gallbladder meridians) according to the direction of flow; they all travel in the same direction, from the front of the head towards the back. Thus, it is important that we comb the hair only in that one direction rather than back and forth. Comb 100 times on each meridian for a total of 500. To increase comfort during the combing process, we can add certain essential oils to the scalp to lubricate the comb. I recommend all-natural herbal oil as we want to avoid any chemicals.

The two bladder meridians begin at the *Jingming* meridian point located on the interior corner of the eyes. Start from just above the eyes (the nose end of each eyebrow) with the toothless, smooth-edged comb or gua sha board and 'comb' upwards, over the forehead to the hair line. Massaging this area is beneficial for people who suffer from high eye pressure and glaucoma in addition to problems associated with the bladder.

The two gallbladder meridians are located on the sides of the head. As with the bladder meridians, start 'combing' from the area near the eyes with a *gua sha* board but from the hairline use a comb or brush and move towards the back of the head in uni-directional strokes. Comb 100 times on each side of the head using an essential oil for lubrication.

I recommend doing this exercise with a family member or friend as it is easier to comb other people's hair than your own. The entire exercise should take only around 10 to 15 minutes and should be done once a day. Again, for more in-depth instructions, please watch the video demonstration at https://www.youtube.com/watch?v=79mu7LOplqQ&feature=youtu.be.

Daily massage 2: Back massage

Hair combing can be done alone, but back massage does require a partner.

As mentioned earlier, the bladder meridian is one of the most important for TCM healthy living. It governs the waste removal process for all the meridians. By improving the fluidity of the bladder meridian we can improve the fluidity of all meridians. The main part of the bladder meridian lies on the back of our body, which is the reason why back massage can be effective in improving fluidity.

Prior to doing the massage, we should examine the back to see if there are any abnormal lumps or areas of rigidity. Lumps signify blockages within the meridian. By checking the location of the lumps using the meridian chart (see Figure 6.3), we can see which of our organs have problems. For example, if we notice a lump near the *Ganshu* meridian point, it is possible that there may be abnormalities in our liver. If a lump is discovered near the *Xinshu* meridian point, then the abnormality may be in the heart. Through practising back massages daily, such lumps may disappear over time.

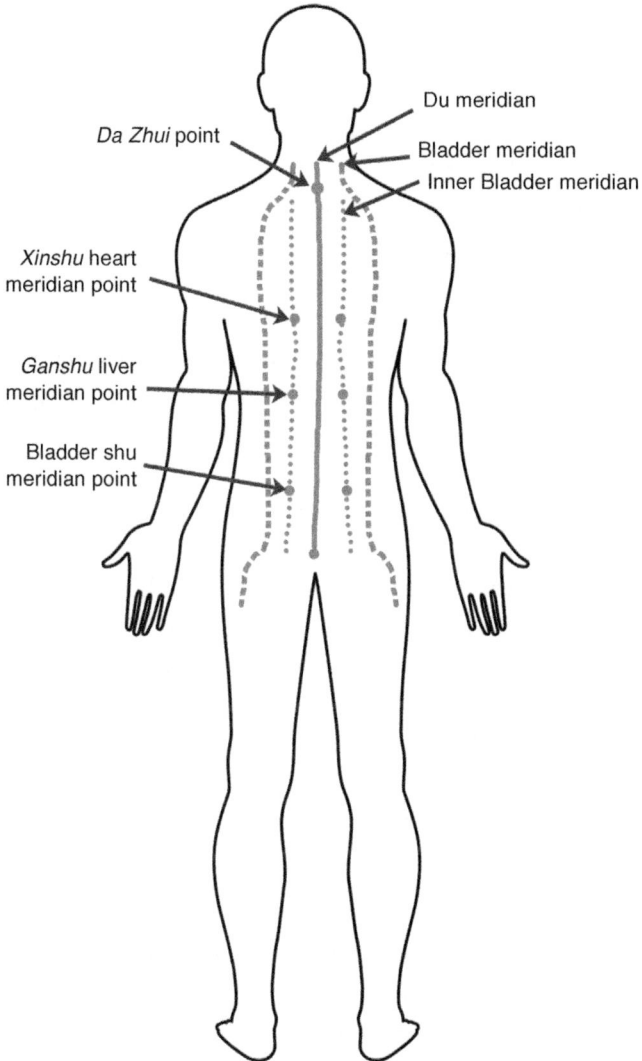

Du meridian

Da Zhui point

Bladder meridian

Inner Bladder meridian

Xinshu heart
meridian point

Ganshu liver
meridian point

Bladder shu
meridian point

Figure 6.3: The back showing the *Du* and bladder meridians and the most important meridian points relating to blockages.

It is helpful if you can find a good essential oil for this massage. In Chinese pharmacies there are many oils that help to improve the fluidity of the meridians and blood flow in the massage areas. It is beneficial to use such oils, but if it is difficult to acquire them, any oil that lubricates the skin will be adequate.

We can either use massage tools such as the popular Gua Sha board (see Figure 6.2) or simply use our hands.

Have the person receiving the massage lie face down on the bed. The person giving the massage stands at the head end, facing the top of the head of the person to be massaged. The back massage can be broken down into three parts: shoulder massage, *Du* meridian massage and the bladder meridian massage. Figure 6.3 shows where these meridians are.

- **Shoulder massage:** Have the person move their body towards the top of the bed until their head is outside the edge of the bed so they can lie completely flat but without squashing their face. Massage the shoulders in this position, working on both simultaneously if using hands. Apply massage oil prior to the massage to avoid damaging the skin. It is normal for the skin to appear red afterwards; it is a sign of poor circulation in the area. Massage 30 strokes on each shoulder, starting from the centre of the neck and moving towards the outside edge of the shoulder.

- ***Du* meridian massage**: Have the person move back down the bed. Apply massage oil and massage the centre of the back (over the spine) starting from bottom of the neck (*Da Zhui* point in Figure 6.3) and going down towards the tailbone. The direction of the massage is very important. We should always massage in a top-down direction as that is the direction in which the meridian flows. Repeat the massage 30 times.

- **Bladder meridian massage**: In the same position, apply massage oil and massage both bladder meridians, which run on either side of the Du meridian. Repeat the massage 30 times on each side. If any area becomes red during the massage, you may massage these areas further after the initial 30 times.

The entire back massage should take around 10 minutes to complete. When practised daily it will achieve noticeable results in two to three months. One of the most common results is a less fleshy back. Most people with poor meridian fluidity in the back tend to have a thick layer of fat in the back area. This massage can effectively remove the fat by improving fluidity and circulation. Other results include better skin quality and complexion as well as a reduction in abnormal skin conditions, such as blackheads and pimples. The reasons for these changes can all be attributed to an improvement in the body's waste removal ability as a result of having a more fluid bladder meridian.

TCM believes that the causes of many chronic diseases originate from the body having a poor waste-removal system. These chronic diseases include several skin conditions, asthma, chronic constipation, some cases of obesity, and more. This massage technique, when practised daily, is an effective method of treating these diseases.

Daily massage 3: Pericardium meridian massage

The two pericardium meridians are located on the centre line of the inner arms (see Figure 6.4). Apply massage oil to the arm and use your thumb. Start massaging from the upper arm (*Tianquan* meridian point) towards the end of the middle finger. Repeat the massage 10 to 20 times on each arm.

As I have said, it is common to see redness appear near the massaged areas. The redness signifies blockage in the meridian and it will appear less often once the fluidity of the associated meridian has improved.

The pericardium meridian massage is an effective way to relieve various heart-related symptoms caused by an increase in pericardial fluid. As I explained on page 87, the pericardium is a double-walled sac containing the heart. Pericardial fluid acts as a barrier and a lubricant between the heart and its surroundings. When there is an increase in pericardial fluid, the excess fluid will hinder the heart's regular functioning. This may result in palpitations, shortness of breath, irregular heartbeat and/or dizziness. An increase in pericardial fluid often occurs when the body is combating disease or performing major self-healing functions. Massaging the pericardium meridians helps the body remove the excess pericardial fluid and restore the heart's regular functioning, thereby eliminating the problem symptoms.

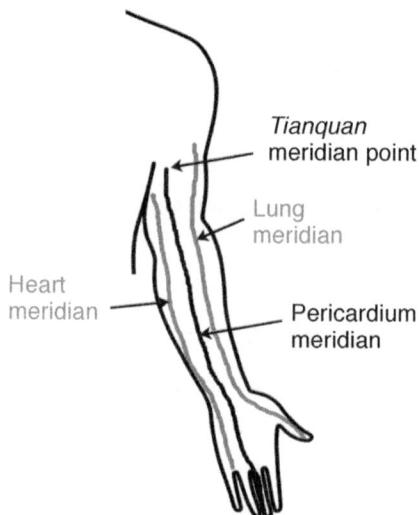

Figure 6.4: The pericardium meridian

Other useful massages

Besides the three daily massages, there are several others that can be done daily or can be useful in particular situations. They are included in the video at https://www.youtube.com/watch?v=79mu7LOplqQ&-feature=youtu.be.

Lung meridian massage

The two lung meridians are located near the pericardium meridians (see Figure 6.4), essentially down the outer edge of the arm when the palm of the had is facing forwards. After the pericardium massage, you can massage the portion of each lung meridian that runs from the elbow to the finger tips. Using your knuckles, gently massage the area about 15 to 20 times by running the knuckles from elbow to wrist.

Massaging the lung meridian can improve the functioning of the lungs and is especially useful when a person has a cold. This massage is also very helpful for people with any type of skin disease.

Gallbladder meridian massage

The gallbladder meridians are located on the exterior of the thighs (see Figure 6.5). Massaging them can improve the functioning of the gallbladder, which increases the person's ability to absorb nutrients. Using a similar technique as for the lung meridians, massage the exterior of the thighs 20 times.

Besides massaging the gallbladder meridian, one can also strike the area with a loosely clenched fist in three or four places, starting at the top of the thigh and working down towards the knee.

Since the release of this book in China in 2005, the gallbladder meridian massage has gained popularity within the Chinese community. The massage is suitable for all ages and can be practised daily.

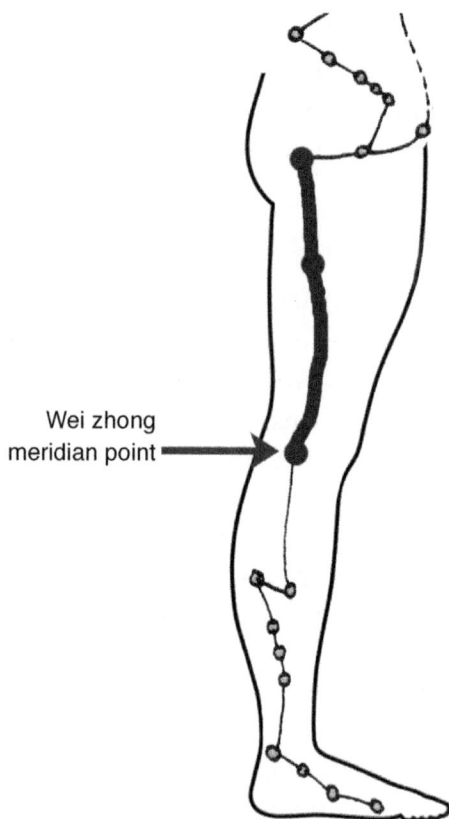

Figure 6.5: The gallbladder meridian in the thigh

Sanjiao meridian massage

The two *Sanjiao* meridians are located on the back of the arms; their location is the direct opposite of the pericardium meridians (see Figure 6.6). Separate the *Sanjiao* meridians into two sections: the upper section which goes from the shoulder to the elbow, and the lower section which goes from the elbow to the fingertips. Massage the upper section using the technique that we used for the lung meridian, with the knuckles of the fist, running them downwards from shoulder to elbow. Massage the lower section of the meridian using the technique that we used for the pericardium meridian, using the thumb, running it downwards from elbow to the end of the fingertips.

The *Sanjiao* massage is useful for alleviating neck and shoulder stiffness.

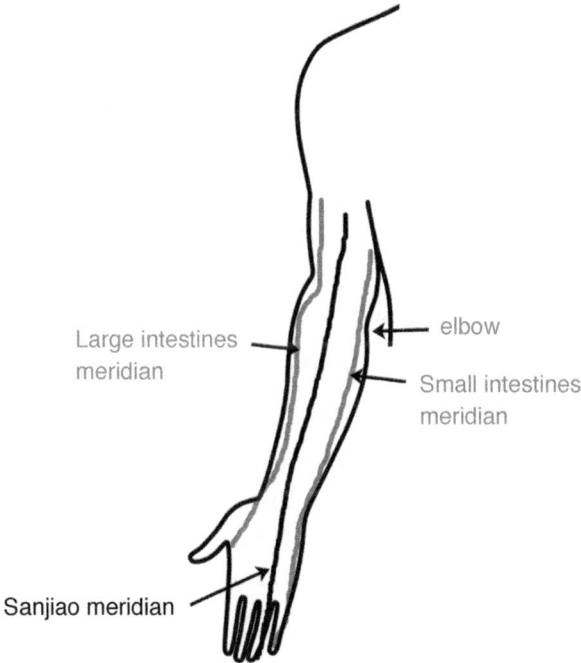

Figure 6.6: The position of the *Sanjiao* meridian on the back of the arm

Summary

- The programme of simple home massages described in chapter 6 and in the video at https://www.youtube.com/watch?v=79mu7LOplqQ&feature=youtu.be when used as a whole on a regular basis can promote self-healing and resilience.

- The programme requires no expertise or training, takes around 15 minutes a day and is good to do with the help of family members.

- Overall the programme removes meridian waste and overcomes blockages in the meridian system.

- Daily simple massage 1: Combing – this massages the five meridians in the head (central Du plus two bladder and two gallbladder meridians).

- Daily simple massage 2: Back – this focuses on the inner bladder meridian that consists of meridian points that link the bladder meridian to other meridians (e.g. heart, liver); unclogging the bladder meridian can slow down aging and combat chronic illness.

- Daily simple massage 3: Pericardium – massaging this meridian in the arm can improve heart symptoms such as palpitations.

- Daily simple massage 4: Other meridians – these include the lung meridian for breathing and combating colds; the gallbladder meridian in the legs; the *sanjiao* meridian in the arms; and the *wei zhong* meridian point behind the knees that helps combat lower back pain.

- Everybody can be empowered by these massage techniques to maintain their own health and allow their bodies to self-heal where necessary.

CHAPTER
7

The future of Traditional Chinese Medicine and its concept of self-healing

With the inevitability of longer life expectancy, proper understanding of how to maintain our health long-term has become increasingly vital to our quality of life. However, properly managing our health is time consuming and difficult without an efficient, systematic set of concepts to guide us. Traditional Chinese Medicine (TCM) provides these concepts and consequently is perfect for the current era.

TCM has always been profound in ways far ahead of its time. Without a fundamental understanding of modern concepts like computer science and systems, it was taught using archaic variable systems that were often more memorised than fully understood. This led TCM to earn the reputation of being unscientific and mystical, a reputation that overshadowed the simplicity and elegance of its logic. When we view the human body as a machine similar to a computer system, concepts like 'Blood' (which holds energy – the 'battery') and 'Qi' (which is the energy – the 'power') as well as energy management (power saving and regulation), become much easier to understand. As body energy is the core of TCM, drawing the parallel between body energy and voltage is an important analogy. Demystifying the concepts of Blood and *Qi* paves the way for a comprehensive discussion of self-healing.

While the idea of utilising the body's own self-healing system to cure diseases is shunned by modern Western medicine, this concept is central to the workings of TCM. The human body is intelligent, and more often than not optimal in its goal of preserving itself in its best state given the circumstances. By understanding the way the body's self-healing system works, we can move up to a healthier state with the least amount of effort and diversion.

I have used the example of gout (page 13) to show that, by understanding what the body is trying to do, we can avoid concentrating our efforts on clashing against our own self-healing system. When modern medicine targets the symptoms of gout as an illness, its medications are designed to combat inflammation (the cause of pain and swelling). The resulting side-effect is that while the inflammation is reduced, the underlying problem – uric acid crystals deposited in joints and tendons – is not removed; the crystals will only pile up more and more when you use medicine to prevent the body from dealing with the underlying problem. What we end up creating using this approach is an untreatable chronic disease.

TCM's logic of self-healing on the other hand, is to recognise that the swelling is part of a self-healing process that is meant to dissolve and remove the uric acid crystals. By recognising and following through the body's self-healing process, attention can be focused on strengthening the body's constitution and energy. To prevent the crystals causing damage to surrounding tissues, the patient must limit movement of the affected joints. The rest of the procedure is simply to rest for three to five days until the swelling goes away and the body's own healing process ends. To prevent uric acid crystals from piling up again, TCM's next step is to review and improve the patient's lifestyle, addressing such factors as lack of sleep, an unhealthy diet, and stress. Contemporary knowledge of nutrition can be used to speed up the healing process. Compared with modern medicine's agonising and ultimately ineffective process, TCM's approach is far more efficient.

The effectiveness of making full use of your self-healing system is the main reason why the popularity of alternative medicine has been on the rise. Modern medicine is highly efficient at handling external problems, such as infectious diseases and injuries. The diseases that it has trouble dealing with are generally those that cut across the conditions, where there is no single link between the symptoms and the disease. For these problems, TCM's advantage compared with other kinds of alternative medicine is in its understanding of how the body's organs funciton and interrelate (the *Zang-Fu* system – see page 51).

When we are trying to understand something as complex as our self-healing system, the *Zang-Fu* system is highly beneficial in providing a methodical approach. The simplicity and well-organised nature of this system allows for easier analysis of the body's complex problems. This leads to a greater understanding of the bigger picture of what the body is trying to do when a certain symptom is observed. At a philosophical level, TCM's *Zang-Fu* system is truly unique in this regard.

With a simplified healthcare philosophy, it becomes easier for us to take responsibility for our own health. In the current mainstream healthcare environment, too much responsibility is left with doctors. Rather than addressing potential hazards while they are still relatively harmless, we continue with erroneous habits until they become significant health risks. Instead, with a better understanding of how our body functions and recognition of the role of the self-healing system, we should be focusing our efforts on taking care of our own health.

The future development of healthcare should involve a reduction in the role of doctors, and a shift towards health 'educators' who function like trainers in a gym. With the convenience of smartphone apps and other similar devices, each individual's health can be regularly monitored. Such health educators could then function as consultants, guiding our health in the right direction. This would not only reduce pain and suffering by treating health problems when they are relatively simple, but also reduce medical costs significantly. Causing massive health problems with unhealthy lifestyles is highly wasteful. It is much more cost-effective to focus our resources on acquiring the knowledge we need to avoid those health problems in the first place.

For such a future, two key sources of objective information are necessary. The first is a means of measuring body energy. The second is a way to assess and monitor energy flow in the meridians. These should be the main parameters for TCM as an objective, verifiable approach to diagnostics and treatment.

Body energy measurement

A system's energy level is one of the most important indicators of its health. For example, an electronic appliance's voltage or a car's petrol gauge are both important indicators of energy level. When the indicator readings are not what they should be, the system concerned is likely to suffer severe malfunction.

The TCM concept of 'Blood and Qi' (see page 21) is regarded as just such an indicator of the body's energy level. A low energy level is then viewed as a primary cause of a variety of illnesses because, with adequate energy, the body's self-healing system would be able to work properly and many of those illnesses would be solved by the body itself. To think about this in reverse, an adequate energy level would imply that the body has enough energy to maintain what needs to be maintained. When your organs are all well maintained, a large proportion of diseases can be avoided. This is why finding ways to measure the body's energy level consistently and objectively is *the* most important goal for developing technology to support TCM.

Modern medicine does not factor the body's energy level into its diagnostics. However, in sports science the basal metabolic rate (BMR), or resting metabolic rate, is very close conceptually to TCM's 'Blood and *Qi*'. BMR uses the amount of oxygen you breathe in and the carbon dioxide you breathe out in a given time interval to determine your energy expenditure at rest.

How useful is this outside sports science? A famous infertility physician in Taiwan with whom I am acquainted uses BMR tests to screen patients. Those with BMR readings outside an acceptable range are refused infertility treatment. Instead, they are instructed to wait and to follow prescribed health recommendations (lifestyle, diet etc) for a few months, until their BMR results improve to meet her requirements. In other words, she only performs infertility treatment on patients with a satisfactory BMR reading. The result is that the rate of success for her fertility treatment is extremely high. Her explanation is that she has already screened out patients whom it would not help. Her method not only saves her patients from paying large medical bills, but also reduces unnecessary pain and suffering.

This physician looks much younger than she actually is. When I asked her how she had maintained her health, her answer was interesting. She said she had closely observed her patients, both those who had successfully achieved pregnancies and those who had remained infertile, and had asked them for details of their lifestyles. She had learnt beneficial behaviour from the successful patients and to avoid the behaviours of those who remained infertile. Her conclusions had been simple. Go to sleep and wake up early, eat foods that are light in flavour, exercise appropriately, cultivate a positive mood and reduce stress. These are in essence exactly the same concepts as those of TCM healthcare.

More and more studies suggest that today's popular lifestyles have seriously detrimental effects on health. With this in mind, many doctors preach lifestyle change to their patients. However, these suggestions are not backed up with any way of measuring the immediate effects of lifestyle changes. If there were a testing parameter that could trend negatively in response to a poor lifestyle and positively to an improved one, it would be easier for doctors to persuade their patients to change.

Meridian data

In the previous section, I talked about the importance of Blood and *Qi* analysis as a TCM parameter. The other important source of data is meridian analysis, giving us information about the state of the meridians. The traditional method for checking a patient's meridian information is for the TCM practitioner to feel the patient's pulse with three fingers on the wrist, with the finding based purely on the doctor's sense of touch. This method of diagnosis has been around for thousands of years, with differing degrees of success depending on the skill of the practitioner. The problems with this method are two-fold. One, it is difficult to learn, and even more difficult to master. Two, there is no way for the patient to differentiate between TCM doctors of differing skills. This is the main reason for the pseudo-science tag that has been given to TCM diagnostics.

Scientists have made many attempts to develop equipment that can replace manual pulse diagnosis, but having to read tiny differences in electrical signals on the human skin, which is full of variability, has made engineering such equipment difficult. Furthermore, to extract

Zang and *Fu* information (see page 51) from an already weak signal has made the difficulty even greater.

As described in greater detail in the Appendix, Dr Yoshio Nakatani discovered in 1951 that meridian points on the skin had different conductivity relative to the rest of the skin. This led to the development of electro-meridian imaging (EMI) for *Ryodoraku* diagnosis (see page 122). The EMI could receive and process signals from the 12 meridians on each side of the body (24 in total). There were no problems with mechanical precision. EMI, from an engineering viewpoint, was far more successful than any previous attempts to replace manual measurement.

However, even though EMI has been around for more than half a century, and is used in various products, it is still not commonly used as a reliable tool for diagnosis. The reasons include:

1. Each time you use the EMI monitor, you need to measure 24 meridian points. The process is therefore complicated and time consuming.

2. Patients expect traditional methods from TCM doctors, often losing confidence in those who cannot or do not perform manual pulse diagnosis.

3. EMI measures conductivity by running a small current through the skin, which causes temporary polarisation, meaning that the meridian points cannot be measured again within a short amount of time. The effect needs to wear off before another test can be done. This makes it impossible to have real-time readings in the way you can from an electrocardiogram, for example. This greatly reduces the scope of the system as well as the credibility of the readings.

4. When measuring the electrical characteristics of the skin,

differences in the pressure applied, skin moisture, skin salinity etc. easily influence the readings. This problem, when compounded with the fact that you cannot obtain measurements in quick succession, makes it difficult to verify the statistical significance of the data.

In 2011, a Taiwanese company developed a new technology, using electromagnetic waves to measure microcurrents in the meridians directly. This new technology does not require running electrical currents through the skin, so it does not have the problems with polarisation that EMI has. This allows for frequently repeated measurements. Results are also not affected by varying levels of pressure, salinity, or moisture in the skin.

When I first discussed their product with the Taiwanese developers, I suggested that they change it from single-point testing to 24-point real-time testing (12 meridians for each side of the body as in EMI). I figured that by bringing the standard of this equipment up to that of the electrocardiograph, the applicability would increase and it could be made to the standards of modern medical equipment.

This real-time EMI – the Meridian Monitoring System described in the Appendix (page 122) – shows the current conditions of the meridians and gives us new, objective insight into changes in the meridians during treatment. It does not, however, reflect their long-term, accumulated condition, so diagnosis cannot be made purely with the data from the real-time EMI. The other methods of TCM diagnosis (see page 23) must also be applied to get a grasp of the patient's long-term state of health and to make deductions about the causes of any illnesses.

Conclusion

As healthcare heads towards the era of big data analysis, TCM's *Zang-Fu* system is the perfect topic for extensive research. The seasonal fluctuations in our bodies' energy levels and meridian patterns, the difference in meridian patterns amongst different age groups, and the body energy and meridian patterns related to chronic illnesses are just the tip of the iceberg in terms of potential research topics. In a time where the applications of AI are being explored, it is the perfect environment for TCM to thrive and grow as a science. Without a doubt, in the near future there will be drastic changes in the way we think about healthcare.

The Meridian Monitoring System (page 122), the Real-Time Meridian Monitoring System (page 123) and the Meridian *Qi* Treatment system (page 123) have all been developed and made available for commercial use in the last decade. As the equipment becomes more popular among TCM practitioners, more patient data can be accumulated in the future. It is my lifelong goal and dream to modernise the diagnostic and treatment methods of Traditional Chinese Medicine. With this new technology, I believe it is possible that one day TCM will be able to provide objective, evidence-based results.

氣 血

APPENDIX

Technology and Traditional Chinese Medicine

In the last two decades, especially in Mainland China, efforts have been made to combine Traditional Chinese Medicine with Western medicine. The 'fusion of East and West', as people call it, has led to the inclusion of TCM in many Western hospitals in China. Patients are diagnosed using standard Western diagnostic procedures (blood tests, X-rays, ECGs etc), but the doctors then prescribe Chinese herbs or TCM treatment methods (such as cupping, acupuncture or massage) rather than Western treatments.

While the combination of Western medicine and Chinese medicine has increased the latter's popularity in China, correspondence between the two fields encounters many problems that limit the effectiveness of TCM treatments. The main problem stems from a difference in the philosophy of diagnosis. Chinese medicine relies on the understanding that human bodily organs are interrelated. As I have described, through the analysis of the relationships between organs, mainly the *Zang* and *Fu* organs, its diagnosis can determine the origin of an illness and formulate a treatment plan aimed at eliminating the origin of the problem rather than temporarily reducing the symptoms. The combination of Western medicine diagnosis with TCM treatment methods or herbs is ultimately disappointing because Western medical treatment prioritises the reduction of symptoms over the elimination of causes.

For example, a patient in a high-pressure, stressful work environment develops a stomach ulcer and experiences pain. When the patient visits a regular Western hospital, the doctor will prescribe ulcer medication. When the same patient goes to visit a hospital that features the New Chinese Medicine, or Chinese medicine with Western diagnostic methods, instead of standard ulcer medication, the patient will receive herbal or TCM treatments. If the same patient goes to a practitioner who uses the TCM diagnostic method, the outcome will be quite different. Firstly, the practitioner will know that the cause of the stomach ulcer is likely to be the stressful work environment, at least in part. Stress is considered a pathogenic factor similar to anger, an emotion governed by the liver. As I have described (see page 53), a diagnostic tool often used in TCM is the Five Elements Theory, which summarises how each *Zang* and *Zang* organ interacts. When a negative effect occurs in one of the elements (metal, for example), it will cause a negative effect in a corresponding element (in this case wood). Wood will negatively affect earth, earth will affect water, water will affect fire, and fire will affect metal, which will affect wood and so the cycle continues. When a negative effect occurs in the liver, which is represented by the element wood, it will cause a negative effect in the stomach, represented by the element earth. Using the Five Elements Theory, the TCM practitioner is able to make a link between the two organs, the liver and the stomach, and come up with the proper TCM diagnosis which focuses on removing the negative effect in the liver, which in turn will remove the symptoms occurring in the stomach. *TCM treatments are meant to be used in accordance with TCM diagnosis.*. In the case of the stressed patient with a stomach ulcer, the proper TCM diagnosis should lead to treatments that are focused on the liver rather than the stomach. At a hospital that combines Western diagnosis with TCM treatment, the patient will receive treatment that focuses on the stomach, which will inevitably be less effective in curing the illness.

To construct the correct method of correspondence between the two fields of medicine, we should first acknowledge the strengths and weaknesses of both. The main strength of TCM is its systemisation of the human body organs and its ability to analyse the relationship between each organ in order to determine the origin of an illness. The main weakness of TCM lies in its lack of objective diagnostic tools. Its diagnostic methods are typically subjective and unquantifiable. It is common for different TCM doctors to make different diagnoses concerning the same patient. Lack of quantifiable data makes data analysis impossible, which means the task of measuring the effectiveness of treatment is difficult.

Western medicine's strength lies in its diagnostic tools. While we should not combine these with TCM treatments, the use of diagnostic tools that are objective and produce quantifiable results is the main area in which TCM diagnosis should strive to improve.

The Meridian Monitoring System

In 1951, Dr Yoshio Nakatani MD PhD developed a method of examining the meridian system by measuring the skin conductivity of the 24 meridian points (also known as *Yuan* points) near the wrists and ankles. He was able to develop a system of diagnostic and treatment methods that utilises electronic readings from these. Over decades of research and clinical testing, Dr Nakatani was able to show that the diagnosis he obtained through his system corresponded accurately to the diagnosis obtained using common TCM methods, such as pulse reading and tongue diagnosis. He named his new method of diagnosis *Ryodoraku* and it has become a popular tool among acupuncturists and general TCM practitioners worldwide.

However, while *Ryodoraku* is a revolutionary method for TCM in terms of diagnostic accuracy and objectivity, it does carry certain limitations due mainly to variations in skin conductivity caused by the environment. In areas of high humidity, *Ryodoraku* readings will differ from those made in areas where the environment is dry. The temperature also has an influence, as skin condition can be influenced by sweating. *Ryodoraku* is also limited in its repeatability; in order to measure the conductivity of the meridian points, an electric current must be passed through the area. The polarity of the measured area will be altered by the electric current, so the user cannot repeat the measurement on that area until its polarity has returned to its original state. This means it is impossible for *Ryodoraku* to repeatedly measure one area in order to observe changes during treatment. (There is more on these limitations on page 115.)

In 2006, a research team in Taiwan developed a new method of electronic meridian diagnosis based on Dr Nakatani's *Ryodoraku*. Their new piece of equipment obtains data by measuring the body's own electrical microcurrent rather than measuring the skin's conductivity. After years of research and experimentation, the new diagnostic equipment, the Meridian Monitoring System, was able to obtain results similar to the original *Ryodoraku* while resolving to some degree the original's limitations. And because the Meridian Monitoring System could measure areas repeatedly, real-time measurement became a possibility. After six years of further research and design, the Real-

Time Meridian Monitoring System was completed, a breakthrough in technology that has brought revolutionary changes to the way TCM diagnosis is conducted. It represents the future of TCM.

By using the Meridian Monitoring System, TCM practitioners can objectively observe the current state of the patient's 12 meridians. After appropriate training, the TCM practitioner can use the data collected by the Meridian Monitoring System to determine more accurately which treatment methods are suitable for the patient. More importantly, the data obtained by the Meridian Monitoring System are quantifiable and can be further analysed and discussed among TCM practitioners. This can promote growth in the knowledge-base of TCM diagnosis and the accuracy and effectiveness of TCM treatment.

Meridian *Qi* Treatment

Just as the Meridian Monitoring System has allowed great advances in TCM diagnosis, the Meridian *Qi* Treatment has done much to improve treatment and restore the benefits of acupuncture.

History of acupuncture and Qigong

Qigong (or the art of cultivation and control of *Qi* energy) has existed in China for thousands of years. In *Huangdi Neijing* (*The Yellow Emperor's Inner Canon*), one of the most influential books of TCM as I have mentioned, methods for practising *Qigong* are described, as well as how the fluidity of *Qi* benefits the human body. Laozi, the author of the *Tao Te Ching* and the founder of Taoism (or Daoism), makes repeated mention in his writings of the existence of *Qi*. The practice of *Qigong* has always been an integral part of the Chinese lifestyle and it was especially important in the past for TCM practitioners.

It is a well-known fact that many of the famous TCM masters in history were also successful *Qigong* practitioners. Some not only practised *Qigong*, but developed ways of using it to cure various ailments. For example, Hua Tuo, one of the most famous TCM doctors in history, created *Wuqinxi* ('The exercise of the five animals') as a method of using *Qigong* to improve the overall health of the internal organs. *Qigong* has long been an integral part of TCM and it is one of the main factors behind the effectiveness of TCM treatments.

In ancient times, acupuncturists were required to practise *Qigong* prior to learning how to use acupuncture needles. When the acupuncturist applies the needle to the patient, s/he should be able to direct his/her *Qi* into the patient's body through the meridian point. This is the main theory used to explain why certain meridian points can influence organs that are not in their immediate vicinity. *Qi* can travel along the meridian and reach different areas of the body.

Unfortunately, most modern acupuncturists no longer practise *Qigong*. As a result, the effectiveness of modern acupuncture pales in comparison with that of ancient times. The acupuncture methods described in the past can no longer produce the results recorded. This is due not to errors of documentation, but rather to the quality of the practitioner. Nowadays acupuncture is mostly used for ailments associated with physical pain and muscle strains. The use of acupuncture in curing chronic diseases is very limited due to its lack of effectiveness. Fortunately, with the introduction of the Meridian *Qi* Treatment, the real benefits of acupuncture can be restored.

Technology that restores the effectiveness of meridian treatment

Meridian *Qi* Treatment uses a special '*Qi* Wafer' to generate *Qi*. By using a specific type of 12-edged crystal, *Qi* can be focused into a beam and, by directing the *Qi* beam at certain meridian points, the state of the meridians can be altered.

The effects of Meridian Qi Treatment can be monitored using the Meridian Monitoring System, making it clear that changes occur in the affected meridians. In this way we can observe changes in the meridians during treatment, which is especially useful in medical research facilities. Together these new technologies provide an opportunity for objective assessment of TCM.

氣 血

Index

acupuncture,
> history of, 123
> sites, arms, 50

author's story, 5-7, 78-81

basal metabolic rate (BMR), 113

bladder meridian, 57, 76, 98, 101
> massage of, 98-100, 103
> waste removal and, 57

Blood and *Qi*, 12, 21-22, 41-43, 70, 109
> analysis of as a TCM parameter, 114

Blood production, 41-43,

chewing, importance of, 93

chronic disease, 53, 111
> causes of, 16
> waste removal and, 103

cold Qi, 31, 39, 67, 80

cold-temperature damage, 29

common cold, 29, 33-35, 39

diagnosis
> TCM approach, 85
>> observation, 23, 61
>> pulse, 84-85, 114
> skin in, 61-2
> TCM versus Western, 34, 119-121

diet, clean v. unclean, 88-90

diet, manner of eating, 93

Du meridian, 98, 101
> massage of, 98-99

electro-meridian imaging (EMI), 115, 122

energy, body, 16-19
> five levels of, 23-26
> how to increase, 41-43
> importance for self-healing, 62, 66
> management of, 64
> measuring, 61-62, 112

Fei Lun, Professor, 55, 56

Five Elements theory, 52-53

Fu organs, 51

gallbladder meridian, 30-31, 42, 98, 106
> massages of,
>> head, 99-100
>> thigh, 105, 106

gout, 2, 13-16, 36, 40, 110

gua sha board, 99

group dining, risks of, 89

gynaecological infections, 90

hair colouring, 76

hair combing massage, 76, 80, 97-100

hair loss, 6, 57, 78-81

heart meridian, 49

high blood pressure, 120

heart disease, 85

Hua Tuo, 124

hypertension, 120

iced water, dangers of, 91-93
infections, 87
  gynaecological, 90
infertility, 113
inflammation, 13-15, 34, 110

kidney system, 79

Laozi, 123
large intestine meridian, 49
lifestyle changes, 16
  measuring the impact of, 114
  symptoms arising from, 62
lung meridian, 32, 33, 49

massages, 97-
  back, 100-3
  bladder meridian, 103
  difference from usual, 54-55
  Du meridian, 102
  gallbladder meridian, 105, 106
  hair combing, 97-100
  lung meridian, 105
  pericardium meridian, 103, 104
  Sanjiao meridian, 107
  shoulder. 102
measurement,
  body energy, 18,
  body energy, objective, 112
  body energy in sports medicine,
    113
  body energy, traditional, 23
  energy flow in meridians,
    objective, 114
  energy flow in meridians,
    traditional, 84-85
Meridian Monitoring System, 122-123
meridian points,
  Jing ming, 99

Tianquan, 103
Yuan, 121
meridians, 47
  as fluid passageways, 54, 74
  blockages of, 100
  data from, 113
  fluidity of, 57, 69
  the twelve, 47-48
  see also specific meridians
Meridian *Qi* Treatment, 117, 125
midnight-moon ebb-flow (*Zi Wu Liu
  Zhu*), 43
monosodium glutamate (MSG), 78

nutrients
  absorption of, 43, 94-95
  importance of, 41-43

obesity, 83
  causes of, 84
  heart disease and, 85-86
  iced water and, 91
  prevalence, 84
  spleen and, 86
organ interaction, 45-48

parasites, 85
pericardial effusion, 85
pericardium meridian, 49, 103, 104
postpartum recovery, 90-91
preventive medicine, 111
product designer's view, 9-11, 13-16
psoriasis, 63, 71-78
  recovery from, 75-78
  redefining symptoms, 75
pulse diagnosis, 84-85, 114

Qi, 21-22
quality v. quantity of life, 13, 109

Quigong, 46
    history of, 123-4

raw fish, risks of eating, 89
Real-time Meridian Monitoring
    System, 123
Ryodoraku diagnosis, 115, 122

saliva, source of cross-infection, 89
Sanjiao meridian, 48-49, 107
Scalp, meridians in, 80, 98
science and TCM, 114
self-healing system, 12, 35, 60-64
    differentiation from illness, 34
    energy levels and, 62, 66
    logic of, 63
    maintenance v. emergency, 65
    meridian fluidity and, 69
    organ repair prioritisation and,
        67-69
    slow pace of, 77
    symptoms caused by, 37, 67-70
    uncomfortable symptoms of, 35
skin as detox pathway, 73
sleep, 42-43, 76, 79
small intestine meridian, 49
spleen, 86-87
    causes of weakness in, 88-91
stomach meridian, 32
stomach ulcer, 120
stress, 16, 24, 120

Taoism/Doaism, 123
Tao Te Ching, 123
TCM
    and science, 114
    as an art, 114
    history of underlying philosophy,
        3-4

TCM v. Western medicine, 11, 27, 111
    body energy measurement, 18
    diagnostic approach, 34, 119-121
    heart disease, diagnosis of, 85
    obesity, understanding of, 84
    psoriasis treatment and, 71-72, 77
    self-healing system, concept of,
        110
    strengths and weaknesses of each,
        121
toxins, external
    food additives and preservatives,
        76
    hair products, 76

voltage of human body, 16-19

waste removal, 57, 37, 87
    bladder meridian and, 100
    chronic illness and, 57, 103
    kidneys in, 91
    meridians in, 56-57
    skin in, 30-31, 73
    symptoms resulting from
        improvement in, 37, 103
Wuqinxi (exercise of the five animals),
    124

Yellow Emperor's Inner Canon, 9, 10, 42,
    67, 123
Yoshio Nakatani, Dr, 115, 121

Zang organs, 51, 111
Zang and *Fu*,
    balance between, 68
    philosophical importance of, 111

Beat Chronic Disease
The Nutrition Solution

By Fleur Brown

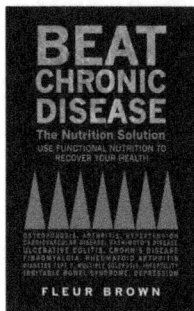

Has anybody looked at ALL your health problems
and ALL the possible underlying causes together?

Fleur Brown, Functional Nutritionist for nearly 25 years,
shares her experience of helping thousands of clients recover
their health, vitality and wellbeing.

She shows you how to:
become your own health detective to
investigate the root causes of your problems

•

take charge of your health holistically

•

take steps to regain your wellbeing and live a
full life without pain or excessive fatigue.

Fleur explains how to apply the principles of functional nutrition to
understand and overcome your health problems based on her extensive
clinical experience and illustrated by detailed case histories. Exploring
the principles for YOU using Fleur's personally developed protocols
is what makes this book a unique resource.

Sustainable Medicine
…whistle-blowing on 21st century medical practice

By Dr Sarah Myhill

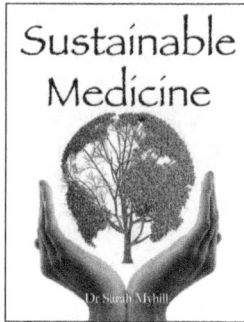

This life-changing book is based on the essential premise that 21st century Western medicine, driven by vested interests, is failing to address the root causes of disease processes. Symptom-suppressing medication and poly-pharmacy are resulting in an escalation of disease and a system of so-called 'health care' which is NOT sustainable.

In *Sustainable Medicine*, Dr Sarah Myhill aims to empower her readers to heal themselves through addressing the underlying causes of their health problems. She presents a logical progression from symptoms to identifying the underlying mechanisms, to the relevant interventions, tests and tools with which to tackle the root causes of their symptoms.

www.hammersmithbooks.co.uk/ product/sustainable-medicine/